SPIKKIN DORIC

SPIKKIN DORIC
A Doric Word Book

Norman Harper

BIRLINN

First published in 2009 by
Birlinn Limited
West Newington House
10 Newington Road
Edinburgh
EH9 1QS

www.birlinn.co.uk

ISBN 13: 978 1 84158 680 9

British Library Cataloguing-in-Publication Data
A catalogue record for this book is available from the
British Library

Typeset in Minion at Birlinn

Printed and bound in Great Britain by Bell & Bain Ltd

FOREWORD

Language is never static. In the ten years since I wrote *Spik o the Place*, the first modern dictionary of the Doric dialect in daily use, some words have fallen further from favour, and some new ones have arisen. When Birlinn hatched the idea of updating the book for the 21st century, I agreed that the time was right and set to work.

Some Doricisms have fallen out of regular use (bleish, sclabdadder), and some that were omitted first time round or have risen into popular speech have been added (neggish, scoosher, tapper).

The result is this dictionary of contemporary Doric, fine-tuned for a new decade with plenty of fresh material. As before, I ask only two things. First, if you are expecting the Doric from 19th-century agriculture, I'm afraid you have come to the wrong place. Those words are all but dead, much as you and I regret that, and their revival is not our purpose.

Second, you might not agree entirely with the spellings or even definitions of certain words, but that's for two reasons. First, there is no great written tradition of Doric, so the variation of spellings is immense. Second, the dialect varies from area to area within the North-east. Moray Doric, Banffshire Doric, Buchan, Formartine, Garioch, Donside, Deeside, Aberdeen and Mearns Doric . . . all are subtly different. I have noted the provenance where possible. Otherwise, you will have to trust me that what you see here is accurate to at least one area of our region.

Finally, thanks to Christopher Riches, who edited this book. He might not be a native speaker, but that was a bonus; he showed not only great patience but brought an outsider's eye for clarity that will help non-natives who want to learn more. Thanks, once again, to the team at Birlinn, who have published me for 15 years. And finally, thanks to my wife, Alison, who brought the coffee and didn't sigh too loudly as I locked myself away for another evening at the computer.

If you wish to contact me or find out about my other books, please visit my website at *www.stronach.co.uk*.

Norman Harper
February 2009

For Rosemary
. . . who has laid down her clipboard for a well-earned
retirement

A few words of guidance for those unfamiliar with our Doric ways

A curious grammatical feature of the North-east dialect is that most concrete and abstract nouns are given their diminutive form. One does not go for a Sunday run, one goes for a Sunday runnie. One does not open a tin of beans, one opens a tinnie. One does not clean the front steps, one cleans the steppies. These diminutives are applied irrespective of the scale or size of the noun which they modify. Thus, a Sunday jaunt from Aberdeen to Inverness, then to Wick, to Durness, down to Fort-William, on to Perth and back to Aberdeen, would amount to more than 700 miles and would still be just 'a fine runnie'.

We also have curious ways of questioning ourselves. A peculiar feature of Aberdonian grammar in which a statement has a rhetorical question tagged on to the end of the original sentence by means of a secondary clause. It is the question part which is given stress, viz: 'He's a handsome man, is he?' 'He wis richt good til his berrens, wis he?' 'She's jist Doon the Toon, is she?' The neatest translation to English form would be to convert the 'is he?', 'wis he?' and 'is she?' to 'isn't he?', 'wasn't he?' and 'isn't she?'

A variation of this is when the speaker asks a question and promptly answers it himself. 'Did ye enjoy yer holidays, ay?' 'Did ye nae find fit ye wis lookin for, no?' 'Are ye burstin for the lavvie, ay?' 'Did she nae offer ye a lift hame, no?'

And when we speak, we put the stress on the last syllable. 'The committee wid like tae thank Mr Robbie Shepherd for his comments.' Note that 'comments' also takes the stress on the last syllable.

A

aa dirt or aa butter
All dirt or all butter, meaning there's never a happy medium; it's always all good fortune or all disaster. This phrase is used especially by self-employed tradesmen lamenting the seasonal nature of their businesses.

aa on ae plate
Describing an insubstantial reward, said most often of someone who works above and beyond the call for an ungrateful or exploitative employer. 'Johnnie works twelve oors a day, sax days a wikk, and disna get nae overtime. He'll maybe get his reward, bit it'll be aa on ae plate.'

aa ower the back
Completely out of control. An Aberdonian expression from the Thirties, when many families stayed in tenements and habitually turfed the children out to play in the back close. In naturally high spirits, the children would race across every square inch of the close, shouting and squealing, seemingly deranged with excitement. Hence, it's a suitable description of any display of uncommonly high spirits

A

verging on complete stupidity. 'Did ye see the clowns on the TV last nicht? Wis thon nae aa ower the back?'

ablow

Underneath. 'Granda disna trust buildin societies or bunks. He keeps his siller in a box ablow his bed.' Note, it can also be used in the phrase **in ablow**, as in: 'There's an affa puddle o ile in ablow yer car, Sandra.'

ace o picks

Ace of spades. This can refer to the playing card, but is heard most often when describing something which is black or profoundly dirty. 'Awa up the stairs and wash yer face. Ye're as black as the ace o picks.'

act feel

Advice on how to generate assistance. The full phrase is 'Act feel and ye'll get a hurl' (*behave as if you're stupid and someone will take pity on you*). 'I canna be bothered cleanin the windaes.' 'Act feel and ye'll get a hurl.'

adee

Wrong or *ado.* A word heard very rarely on its own; more often as part of the friendly query: 'Fit's adee?', meaning: 'What's wrong?'

affa

This carries a dual meaning, depending on context. It can be an adverb (*terribly*) or an adjective (*excessive*). In either case, it is an all-purpose Doric word which is used to apply emphasis. No one is ill in the North-east; we are 'affa nae weel'. There are no thunderstorms; we have 'an affa day o rain'. We don't break the speed limit; we 'ging at an affa lick'.

afflet
A small water-drainage channel dug from a roadside down into a ditch. 'We were walkin hame in the dark and Horace trippit in an afflet and broke his leg.'

ages wi
Equivalent in years. 'Graham's quine is ages wi oor David.'

aiblins
Perhaps, maybe. 'We'll get fower fowk in the car wi their cases, aiblins five.'

aipples
A sharp rebuff to anyone whose approaches are unwelcome. The full phrase is 'I've hid aipples aff your cairtie afore', meaning, *once bitten, twice shy.* 'Can I interest ye in this revolutionary new vacuum-cleaner?' 'Aipples.'

ale
Any soft fizzy drink. 'Mam, can I hae a drink o ale?' 'Awa doon til the shoppie for a bottle o ale.' Also known as Dazzle in some parts of Banffshire and Buchan, after the North-east's own version of cola. Dazzle, sadly, shuffled off the supermarket shelves several decades ago.

ask for
To inquire after someone's health. 'Tell yer dad I wis askin for him.' Doric-speakers would use the word **speirin** instead of 'askin'.

A

A

'at blaiks aa

That beats everything. 'So yer wife's expectin saxtuplets, Ernie. Weel, weel, 'at blaiks aa.'

aul claes and porritch

Old clothes and porridge. At the end of a holiday, when all the spending money has gone, one observes ruefully that one must return to the daily grind. 'Back til the work the morn. Back tae aul claes and porritch.'

ava

At all. End-of-sentence stress, with the accent on the second syllable. 'Foo money straaberries were ye left wi efter the kids went hame on Sunday?' 'Neen ava.' You can also substitute **ata** for 'ava'.

awa fae't aa

Away from it all. Dead, in other words. 'That's him awa fae't aa noo.' If the death is thought to have been a merciful release, someone will observe philosophically, 'He's better aff awa.'

awa ye go

I don't believe you. 'Yer mither's a size twelve? Awa ye go.' As an alternative, you might try: 'Awa and burst.'

ay-ay

A greeting used more as an acknowledgment in passing, with no reply expected. 'Ay-ay, Wullie. Fine day.'

B

ba up

This has no literal translation, but is short for the Aberdonian expression, 'ba up on the slates', meaning *something which has gone badly wrong*. 'I said I needed a plumber here yesterday morning.' 'Sorry, sir, the hale office his been ba up since the wikkend.' It is derived from a children's backyard kickabout game. If the ball got stuck on a roof and couldn't be retrieved, the game came to an abrupt end and everyone had to shuffle home. The 'ba' had gone 'up' on the slates.

bachles

Shoes beyond repair. The 'ch' is pronounced as in 'loch'. 'I peyed thirty poun for this sheen. Twice on and that's them bachles already.'

baffies

House slippers. 'There's nithing sae comfortin efter a hard day's wark as a soak in the bath, pittin on yer goon and shochlin in yer baffies.' Some parts of the North-east know baffies as **safties**. Safties (qv) are also sandwich buns or stupid people.

B

bakin
The act of cooking pastries and cakes in the home, but also *the collective noun for anything thus produced.* 'Come awa in for a fly cup, Gertie. I've nae lang finished a bakin.'

bannocks
Large thin pancakes (as opposed to girdle scones or drop scones). Bannocks are also double chins. 'Elsie wid hae a bonnie face if it wisna for aa thon bannocks it's cairryin.' Bannocks can also be oatcakes in some parts of the North-east.

bap-face
One whose complexion is alarmingly pale. 'What a bap-face Wullie hid fin he cam oot o hospital.' There is also a school of thought that a bap face is a soft, pudgy and stupid-looking face.

bap feet
Flat-footed. 'Oor Ed wisna in the Army durin the waar. They widna tak him because o his bap feet.'

bap nose
An exceptionally squashed nose. This can be congenital or, more frequently, as a result of excessive fighting or alcohol consumption. It is named for its resemblance to a sandwich bun. 'The Morrisons' aulest loon wid be real presentable if it wisna for his bap nose.'

bap poodin
Bread-and-butter pudding, to anyone else.

bappit

Collided. 'I wis mindin ma ain business at the traffic-lichts and some gype bappit intae the back o me.'

bare nakit

Starkers. 'There's far ower mony bare-nakit wifies on the TV nooadays. Gie's back Minnie Caldwell, I say.'

barkit

Excessively dirty. 'Foo lang hiv ye been weerin that sark, Jim? Yer collar's barkit.'

bate

Defeated. 'Their centre-half jinkit left, jinkit richt and syne haimmered it in. That wis them bate.'

beamer

Blush. 'I found them canoodlin at the back o the bikesheds, and she took a richt beamer.'

beens

Bones, not the tinned vegetable. Hence: 'I'm affa troubled wi ma beens,' is a sign of rheumatism, not gastric embarrassment.

beardie

A peculiar expression of affection between a North-east father and his children, possible only when he is unshaven. The child is grabbed and the father's face is rubbed vigorously along the child's cheek. When concluded, the father laughs uproariously and the child goes

B

B in search of a bucket of ice, a tub of calamine lotion and a shoulder upon which to cry. Affection is apparently a difficult concept for North-east fathers. Hence: 'Why have you come to school with your head swathed in bandages, Alfred?' 'Got a beardie fae ma dad last nicht, miss. He loves me really.'

Bennachie bap
Sweet bun worked into a pronounced conical peak and sprinkled with that form of confectioner's sugar which resembles small hailstones. Very popular until the late 1960s, but now made by only a very few family-owned bakeries. Bennachie is central Aberdeenshire's most prominent and celebrated hill. 'Sees a half-dizzen o yer Bennachie baps.'

berrens
Aberdeen word for children, deriving from the city's curious two-syllable pronunciation of the Scots 'bairns'. 'Ma man and me dinna bother muckle wi Christmas. Well, Christmas is for the berrens.'

bick
A bitch. Used of dogs, of course, but also of humans. In the human context, it is rarely derogatory or uttered in anger. It is used most often as a term of affection and sympathy directed at an unmarried mother, as in: 'Ach, weel. A bick's aye the better o a pup.' (*A bitch is always better to have had a pup.*)

bicyclin sark
Sunday-best shirt. The phrase is still used widely and derives from

the days when farm servants would dress up to go out on a day off and the only transport available was the bicycle.

B

bide
Stay at. 'I bide at New Pitsligo.' Bide is not a synonym for **come fae**. One bides wherever one happens to be living at any given moment. One comes fae the place where one was brought up. The distinction is lost on many. 'I bide at New Pitsligo, bit I come fae Cruden Bay.'

bidey-in
One who co-habits. 'Erchie says he mairriet her in South Africa, bit I hinna seen a ring. I doot she's jist a bidey-in.'

bigsy
Snobbish. Used more often of women than men, hence: 'Mina's that bigsy, she thinks she farts Chanel No. 5.'

biled dry
Said of someone who is past being merely exhausted and is near to collapse, either through hard labour or hard liquor. 'Awa hame tae yer bed, min. Ye're biled dry.'

biled ham
Funeral tea. So named because one of the staples of the post-inter-ment refreshments in the North-east has always been a boiled-ham salad or boiled-ham sandwich. 'I saw ye at Wullie's funeral the ither day, bit I didna see ye at the biled ham.' 'No, I left efter the service. I wis that cummat (qv) I cwidna even hae managed the beerial, let aleen the biled ham.'

B

bilin
Any pot of vegetables which has been cooked, but said usually of potatoes. 'Come roon for yer denner, Isa. I've a bilin o new tatties and butter.'

birdie's maet
Birdfood. The little crusty lumps which must be brushed from the eyelashes and corners of the eyes after a night's sleep. 'Awa and wash yer face again, Donald. Yer een's still cakit wi birdie's maet.'

birse
Derives from bristle, meaning to be irked or angered. The most common context relates to dogs. 'Bide weel back fae that rottweiler, Sadie. Ye can see its birse is up.' It can apply also to short-tempered women. 'I feel sorry for Sammy. His wife's birse is aye up, and him sic a quaet chiel.'

blaa
A boaster or *a windbag.* 'Davie's cousin's hame fae America. We've heard aboot his big cars and his big hoose and his sweemin-pool and his fittit kitchen. What a blaa.' An older North-easter would dismiss such a person as **a bleeter o win**.

blaad
To spoil or damage. Illustrated best by a story which John Duff, of Braemar, once told Robbie Shepherd and me about the young lad turning up at a home at Braemar to take the daughter of the house to a dance. Her father bade them farewell and, as the young couple were walking down the garden path, advised the boy: 'Noo dinna blaad the lassie.'

black affrontit

B

Profoundly embarrassed. The 'black' alludes to the blush on the victim's face, which was supposedly so red that it turned purple, then almost black. 'Foo wis I tae ken she wis stannin ahen me aa the time? I wis black affrontit.'

blackening

A pre-wedding custom in which the friends of the bride and groom kidnap them, cover them in treacle, feathers, paint and other hard-to-remove substances, then parade them through their communities on the back of a lorry, sounding horns and flashing lights. Now rare, perhaps because this largely good-natured custom took an alarming turn in the 1970s when some victims were stripped naked and handcuffed to street lights. And there, my lord, rests the case for my clients' defence.

blaik

Shoe polish or dubbin. Irrespective of the nugget's colour, it is always referred to as blaik, hence: 'Grocer, hiv ye a tinnie o broon blaik?'

blate

Shy. 'Ma sister speired at me the day if we'd peyed aff wir mortgage. She's nae as blate as she eese'd tae be.'

bleezin

Drunk. 'He wis that bleezin last nicht they took him hame in a bucket.' Or: 'He spent sae muckle o his life bleezin that they canna hae the funeral at the Crem, for it wid tak a wikk tae pit oot the fire.'

B

bleish
Sudden profusion, but used mostly of rainstorms. 'That's the last time I ging oot athoot a brolly. I wis catched in a bleish o rain.' Or: 'Isn't that bleish o poppies richt bonnie?'

blin drift
A blizzard so fierce that visibility is down to zero. 'Ye canna leave noo, John. It's blin drift oot there.'

blin lump
Pimple or boil at the sore stage just before it has begun to show and erupt. 'I canna sit doon, thanks aa the same. I've a blin lump.'

blink afore a drink
That peculiar watery sun one gets shortly before a shower of rain during a North-east autumn. 'Fit's the weather deein? 'Och, a blink afore a drink.'

bloomers
A puff-pastry biscuit as big as the palm of a woman's hand. The item is smeared with sweet yellow or pink icing and is shaped like a pair of bloomers hanging on a washing-line. 'Fit will we hae wi wir fly cup, Ina?' 'Oh, they dee affa tasty bloomers in this caffy.' 'I'll hae a Kit-Kat if it's a' the same tae yersel.' See also **coo's fit**.

Bob's
Robert Gordon's College or, occasionally, the Robert Gordon University. Not a term which is likely to be well received by the

governors of either educational institution, but nevertheless one which is widely used by pupils, students and throughout the city. 'And has Mr McShuggle retired from Bob's yet?' 'A Bob's education fairly sets ye aff on life's lang road.'

bondie

Bonfire. 'That's the mannie next door put up anither bondie and ma washin's aa smokit.'

bosie

A voluptuous embrace. Used most often to comfort distressed children. 'Skinned yer knees, ma wee lamb? Come ower here for a bosie.' Derives from 'bosom', and the word can also be used of the female anatomy in the same context. 'Skinned yer knees? Come intae ma bosie and that'll mak it better.'

bothyin

Any man looking after himself temporarily at home while his wife or girlfriend is working, holidaying, visiting relatives or otherwise detained away from base is said to be bothyin. Derives from the days when farmworkers looked after themselves in the farm bothy. 'Yer hoose is an affa sotter, Alick.' 'I'm bothyin aenoo. The wife's awa tae Dunbar for the wikkend.'

bradie

North-east version of the Forfar bridie. The recipe is pretty much the same – a pastry parcel filled with ground meat – except that the North-east version is a little smaller.

B

braakfist

Literally *breakfast,* but also *someone who has no dress sense.*
Derived presumably from 'a dog's breakfast'. 'Check Rab ower at the
bus stop. Fit a braakfist.'

bree

Any liquid pressed out of a solid. Thus, the whey that drips out of a
cheesecloth is bree; the liquid screwed from wet socks after a day's hill-
walking is bree, and the water left behind after any pan of vegetables is
cooked is bree. The liquid content of a midden or a byre is **sharn bree**.
To drain the cooking water from a pan of vegetables turns bree into a
verb, as in: 'Claire, awa and bree the tatties' (but see below to make sure
you are not misunderstood). What a multipurpose word.

bree the tatties

Urinate. 'Weel, gentlemen, if ye'll excuse me for a mintie, I'll awa
and bree the tatties.'

breether

Nothing to do with a short rest; *this is the Banffshire word for
brother.* 'Ma breether's got a rare new job wi the Watter Boord.'

breid

Bread, obviously, but in Doric *'breid' is mainly oatcakes.* 'Fit are ye
haein for yer tea, Jimmy?' 'Ach, I couldna be bothered cookin, so I'd
jist some breid and cheese.'

brikks

Trousers. 'Stop the car, Ina. That's the loon spewed a' ower ma Sunday
brikks.'

Broch

B

The North-east's nickname for the Aberdeenshire fishing port of Fraserburgh, but also the Moray port of Burghead, 70 miles west along the Moray Firth coastline. Inhabitants of both are known as Brochers. 'The Brocher quines are fine quines.'

broonie

Any obsequious person who sucks up to authority in the cause of self-advancement (and we all know several of those). 'That's an affa quick promotion young Ian's got, isn't it?' 'He's a bit o a broonie, hid ye nae noticed?' It derives presumably from **brown-noser**, meaning that the individual is not shy of sticking his/her nose up the boss's behind if it results in a title. Such people are also **sooks**.

brose

Oatmeal and salt, mixed vigorously with boiling water. Once the staple diet of all North-east farmworkers, this thick, cloying gruel differs from porridge in that the only heat in the process is derived from the boiling water, so there is very little cooking, as such. Must be stirred thoroughly and quickly to avoid lumps, although many elderly North-easters insisted that the lumps were best. The stirring was done traditionally with a spoon handle. The bowl of the same spoon was later used to eat the mixture. Sunday brose was usually topped off with cream. Most men insisted that the best brose was the brose they made for themselves and that any third-party concoction was a pale imitation of the real thing. Hence 'a man steers his ain brose best'.

brosey

Of burly physical appearance. An English-speaker might say 'strapping'. 'Araminta's got hersel a brosey chiel for her latest

B

fiancy.' A young woman of burly physical appearance is said to be 'a brosey deem'.

brunt
Burned. Cakes can be brunt. One can be brunt from lying too much in the sun. But the most common contemporary use of brunt is demonstrated best in the story of the small boy who turned up late for school. When his teacher asked why, he said: 'Ma faither got brunt es mornin, miss.' 'Oh, I'm sorry to hear that. Was it serious?' 'Ay, they dinna muck aboot at the crematorium.'

bubble
To cry. 'That's Kylie surely split up wi her boyfriend for the sivventeenth time. She cam hame fae the school and went rinnin up the stairs bubblin.'

bubbles
Nasal discharge of the peculiarly liquid variety exclusive to children. 'Come ower here, Jason, and grandma'll dicht yer bubbles.'

bucket
An excess of drink. Someone bordering on alcoholism is said to 'tak an affa bucket'.

buckie
Any normally shy person who suddenly does something which draws attention to himself is said to be 'comin oot o his buckie'. A buckie is *a whelk*, and anyone familiar with the habits of a live whelk will understand the metaphor.

B

bugga

A bag of. 'Jean, that new frock maks ye look lik a bugga cats awa tae be droont.' A child who cannot be persuaded to sit still is said to behave 'lik a bugga rats'.

buggerin

Not a sexual offence, but *a particularly severe chastisement.* 'I got an affa buggerin fae ma boss this mornin.'

bum

Not the human hindquarters, but *a verb meaning 'to boast'.* 'Mair than five meenits in Elsie's company and I feel like screamin. She's aye bummin aboot her femly.'

bunnet

Headgear of the elderly male. 'I see Jim's got a new reid bunnet. It matches his een.' A particularly big and floppy example may be said to be a **doolander**, meaning that it would be wide enough for a doo (pigeon) to land. Also *any elderly man wearing a flat cap.* 'Fit wye are we stuck in a queue o sivventeen cars traivellin at twinty-fower mile an oor?' 'There'll be a bunnet drivin the car at the front.'

burst

Unsuccessful. 'Only twa numbers on the Lottery this wikk. The game's a burst.' Also, *to buy something with a large-denomination banknote.* 'I doot I'll hae tae burst this twenty-poun note.' And *to cut the first slice from some well-presented pie.* 'It's a shame tae burst a new pavlova.'

buttery
The key to a quintessential North-east breakfast. Flour, lard and salt are mixed and cut into random shapes roughly three inches in diameter. They are baked and the results can be spread with butter or margarine, jam or syrup.

byke
A nest, usually of wasps, sometimes of bees. 'Gary wis in amon lang grass and kickit fit he thocht wis a fitba. It wis a wasps' byke. He gets oot o hospital next month.'

byoch
Bring up wind. This verb can also be a noun. Both are clearly ono-matopoeic, as you'll understand if you try saying it. 'Granda tried a suppie pasta for his tea and he's been byochin in front o the TV aa nicht.' See also **rift**.

by-the-way
A Glaswegian. Not much puzzle here; this affectionate term for the sons and daughters of the Dear Green Place was coined because of their alleged fondness for 'by the way' as a suffix to many conversa-tional sentences, viz: 'That wis nivver a penalty, ref, by the way.' In the interests of balance and national harmony, I should admit that Glas-wegians are said to refer to Aberdonians as **Furryboots**, allegedly because of our citizens' curiosity about strangers, as in: 'Furryboots are you fae?'

C

ca
To propel. 'Ca that barra o earth ower tae the flooer beds.' 'Ca twa mair nails intae that plank jist tae be sure.' Also, *to transport.* 'Henry Thomson ca's beasts aa ower Scotland in his cattle floats.'

ca a man till his grave
Enough to kill someone. Could be used of any wearying situation, I suppose, but used most commonly in wartime Aberdeen of a woman who liked to play the field while her husband was away in the Services. Older Aberdonians still use it of flighty females. 'That lassie's jist like her grunnie. Baith o them wid ca ony man till his grave.'

cackit up
Charged. 'The grocer cackit me up twa poun for a half-dizzen peaches.'

caddis
Fluff, dust and other domestic detritus, usually in inaccessible places. 'That bedroom hisna seen a Hoover in months. Ye should see the caddis aneth his bed.' Some people in the course of my researches

C

suggested that it also referred in the modern context to *bellybutton fluff,* but I suspect that was stretching the definition somewhat.

cairry
An off-licence carryout or *a helping hand with a burden.* 'Get's a cairry o a dizzen exports.' 'Wid ye gie's a cairry doon the stairs wi this aul bedstead?'

calved
See **drappit**.

cantrips
In medieval Aberdeen, these were *witches' spells,* occasionally cited in charge sheets for court. Now, they are more likely *capers* or *mischief.* 'Fit like cantrips is that loon o yours up til noo? He let doon aa ma tyres last wikk.'

cappie
Ice-cream cone. 'Awa doon til the shoppie and get's a coupla cappies.'

Carl-Doddie
*A particular form of rib grass (*Plantago lanceolata*) which North-east children use to play a game similar to conkers.* Each player holds a stalk and takes alternate turns to try to knock the head off the other person's grass. The name is more than 250 years old, dating from the time of Bonnie Prince Charlie (Carl) and King George II (Doddie).

cartoon

Container for holding liquids or loose items. Nothing to do with 'Porky Pig' or 'Tom and Jerry', but the North-east's version of carton, I suppose. 'I see they're even sellin soup in cartoons noo.'

casher

The linchpin of the black economy, this is a job which does not appear in any accounts but, rather, is paid for in cash. 'Is this an official job, Wullie, or a casher?'

cassie

A granite road-paving stone. Aberdeen suffered a 1960s orgy of removing these distinctive paviors or tarring them over them on the dubious grounds that drivers deserved more comfort. Now, the best remaining examples are the southern end of Huntly Street and a few roads in Old Aberdeen. Poor show.

cat's sookins

A particularly lank hairdo. 'Ethel peyed aa that money for a perm and it's come oot lik cat's sookins.' An agricultural equivalent is: 'Hair lik straa blaain aff a midden.' See also **hingin mince**.

cattie's faces

Item of North-east bakery popular until the 1960s. A sweet bun roughly 12 inches in diameter was marked into eighths before baking. When pulled from the oven, it was sprinkled with sugar and each eighth could be torn off cleanly and sold individually. The resulting triangular shape of each piece was not unlike a cat's face. 'I'll tak twa bradies, a tattie scone, fower French cakes and twa cattie's faces.'

C

CBE
A lazy person. 'There's Ernie Buchan, CBE.' The CBE stands for Canna Be Ersed (*can't be bothered*).

chaa yer lugs
Chew your ears. Usually the first sign of a spat developing, when one party becomes increasingly exasperated with the other party's conversation, manner or boasting and erupts with: 'Awa and chaa yer lugs!'

a change o loaf
Often used to sum up a less-than-successful day out, whereby the highlight was the purchase of a loaf at the destination town's bakery. 'Weel, I've hid better days oot, bit at least it wis a change o loaf.'

chappin
Knocking. Used in the game of dominoes by any player who cannot make a move with the tiles left in his hand, but also increasingly used of anyone who has reached an impasse. 'We've burst twa tyres, run oot o petrol and we're twelve mile fae the nearest village. We're chappin and nae mistake.'

chatramafaikie
Thingummyjig. Banffshire's stopgap noun for anything which doesn't spring readily to mind. 'Far did ye get thon chatramafaikie in yer front gairden?'

check
Encouragement to observe something surreptitiously, usually

because it's a likely source of humour. 'Check the boy's haircut.' 'Check the dame's frock.'

C

chipper
Chip shop. Always 'the chipper', never 'the chippie'. 'That new manager at the chipper changes his fat ilky sax month whether it needs it or no.' North-east chippers are responsible for such delights as pineapple fritters, haggis suppers, mock chops and the quintessential 1990s delicacy, the deep-fried Mars Bar, although the supposed ubiquity of the fried Mars has been dreadfully overplayed.

choobs
The human insides, otherwise known as guts. Derives from 'tubes'. 'I've been up aa nicht, doctor. Terrible bothered wi ma choobs.' Less polite society refers to this as **poodins**.

Christmas
A gift given on December 25. Few North-east people receive Christmas presents. We receive 'wir Christmas', as in: 'Fit did ye get for yer Christmas, Gibby?' A similar all-purpose inquiry would be: 'Wis Sunty good tae ye?'

chuckies
Small granite stones used to surface driveways throughout Scotland. Almost all come from quarries around the North-east. They may be grey or pink and come in several sizes. 'It'll tak twa larryloads o chuckies tae cover yer yard, missus.'

C

chucks
Choux pastry. Derived, presumably, from pronouncing the word as it looks. 'I prefer Chalmers' chocolate eclairs. Their chucks disna taste o lard.'

chuddie
Chewing-gum. 'There's nithing as orra as lassies chaain chuddie in the street.'

chum
To seek a favour. 'If ye chum Bob, he'll maybe gie ye a shot o his rotavator.'

claa far it's nae yokie
Scratch where it isn't itchy. Said of anyone who has been taken down a peg or two, or who has been given cause to think twice about himself and his behaviour. 'That'll gaur him claa far it's nae yokie.'

clae-davies
Coarse-cloth trousers favoured by older generations of farm-workers because of their durability. 'See Erchie's clae-davies? He's worn them since he got them at Heppie's in the year o the Coronation.'

claik
Gossip, or one who gossips. 'Fit's yer claik, Ina?' 'Dinna set me next tae Mrs Farquhar; she's an affa claik.' Along most of Donside, the word 'claik' becomes **sclaik**, defined in exactly the same way.

C

clap

To pet or stroke an animal. 'Awa and gie the doggie a clap, dearie. On ye go, it winna hurt ye.'

clappit in

Anyone who has removed his false teeth is said to have a clappit-in face.

clappit thegither

Thrown together. Used mostly of sandwiches ('Twa bits o loaf spread wi jam and clappit thegither'), but also used for anything which has been prepared carelessly. 'James, your ink exercise is one of the worst this school has seen. Simply clappit thegither, if I may say so.' And: 'I doot she got dressed in the dark this mornin. Her claes wis jist clappit thegither.'

clart

As a noun, this is *farmyard mud.* As a verb, it means *to plaster on thickly.* Thus, the noun: 'Ye'll need yer weldies (qv) oot in the fairm close the day; there's an affa clart.' And the verb: 'Thon deemie clarts on her make-up lik plaster.' Note that a particularly stupid person is said to be 'as thick as clart in a bottle', which is very colourful, but I'm not sure what it means. Note that anyone with muddy shoes would be admonished with: 'Yer beets is clartit in dubs' (*Your boots are plastered with mud*). Since clart and dubs mean the same thing, this is an example of North-east tautology, or North-east emphasis, depending on your point of view.

cleg

Horse-fly. An insect to be avoided at all costs for its painful bite

C

which leaves a permanent mark. Many North-east inhabitants can point to raised pale spots and tell a tale of a cleg bite 40 years before.

clockie
A prominent fixture at the Beach Ballroom, Aberdeen. Beaux and belles usually agreed to meet each other 'aneth the clockie' prior to an evening's dancing. This was not always an astute arrangement. So many couples agreed to meet aneth the clockie that often hundreds of lost souls were milling about there looking in vain for their clicks, while the dance floor inside remained comparatively barren. Note that in some parts of rural Aberdeenshire, a clock is still referred to as a **k-nock**. 'Fit's the time, Jean? I canna see the k-nockie fae here.'

clockin
Clucking. A broody hen is said to be 'a clockin hennie', but the word can also be used of a fussing old gossip who can't stop talking. 'Sorry I'm late; I fell in wi the wifie Robertson doon the road and ye ken fit she's like for clockin.' This probably led to the Scots variation, **claikin** (qv). Also, any spinster who feels that life and men are passing her by and is desperate for an engagement ring is said to be 'clockin'.

clypie-clypie clashbags
Playground cry of outrage, always directed at the class telltale or teacher's pet, usually one and the same person.

coalie-back
Piggyback. This Aberdonian word is derived from the days of street coalmen carrying sacks of coal on their backs. 'Ye've been oot on that

back green giein the kids coalie-backs for the last twa oors. Ye're a bigger bairn than they are.' See also **horsie-back**.

Cocky Hunter's

Celebrated Aberdeen emporium. It lay just beyond the eastern end of Union Street and its stock was displayed in no particular order so that, even on good days, it looked as if a bomb had hit. The store has long since closed and the site has been redeveloped but, even now, any home or office which badly needs tidying up is said to 'look lik Cocky Hunter's'. The name lives on in a pub at the other end of Union Street.

Codona's

A funfair. The family name of the company which operates the funfair at Aberdeen Beach and which can claim several crowd-pulling attractions. Now used increasingly by many Aberdonians as a generic term for any fairground, funfair or theme park. At this rate, it won't be long before North-east tourists return from Florida or California reporting that they spent most of their time in 'thon Codona's wi the Mickey Moose'.

come ower ye

Befall you. 'Drive slow and nithing'll come ower ye.' Any child who is crying bitterly for no apparent reason will be told: 'Michty, michty. Fit's adee? There's nithing comin ower ye.'

connach

To spoil or *damage.* 'Dinna leave the milk oot in the sun ower lang or it'll connach.' 'If ye keep giein that dog treats ye'll connach it.' 'Ye rode that clutch ower lang and now it's connacht.'

C

C

contermacious

A wonderful Doric word for *difficult* or *obstinate*. 'I widna bother sikkin a len o Geordie's car. He'll tak great delight in sayin no. He's aye been contermacious.' Some lexicographers suggest that it is one of the few Doric words to derive directly from English . . . in this instance the English word *contumacious*.

Co-opie loaf

Pregnant. Bread from the old Co-operative Society bakery in Aberdeen was said to be unusually doughy and liable to swell in the stomach. Hence, a woman in the early stages of pregnancy might be hailed with: 'Fan are ye due? Or is it Co-opie loaf?' That's the Aberdeen expression. The rural one is: **'Hiv ye been aetin new tatties?'**

coorse

Bad, coarse or *awkward*. Another multipurpose Doric word, illustrated best by examples. 'He's been coorse the hale holidays. I'll be gled fin the school starts again.' 'This is gey coorse material for curtains. Hid they nithing bonnier?' 'Gie's the little spanner ower here, this nut's real coorse tae shift.'

coo's fit

Cow's foot. Another name for the pastry-and-icing confection otherwise known as **bloomers** (qv). As well as the shape resembling a voluminous pair of drawers hanging on the washing-line, its outline looks equally like the imprint of a cloven hoof in mud. 'I'll tak half a dizzen coos' feet and three o yer baps, baker.'

C

coorse as cat's dirt

Utterly foul. What was once the most pervasive and malodorous contamination known to North-east farm wives, cat poop, lives on in this expression for anything and anyone that is decidedly less than appealing. 'Gweed kens fit wye he took up wi her; she's as coorse as cat's dirt.'

coppit bonnie

Caught red-handed. 'Ye tell me ye were aff work wi a sair back, and here ye are bungee-jumpin.' 'Ay, boss, that's me coppit bonnie.'

coup-the-ladle

Playground see-saw. 'Ronnie fell aff the coup-the-ladle and clattered his heid aff the cement. Efter extensive tests at the hospital, it's been scientifically proven that his IQ's up twenty-nine points.' The 'coup' is pronounced 'cowp'. Despite best researches, none of my contacts has any idea of the derivation. It might have something to do with ladling soup from a broth pot and spilling the contents, but I'll take advice.

cove

One of many Banffshire words for *an individual*, or *a chiel*. 'Far are ye gaun the day, cove?' See also **gade, gadgie** and **min**.

crackit chuntie

Damaged chamberpot. Anyone whose singing voice is not what it might be is said to have 'a voice lik a crackit chuntie'. The same voice might also be described as **lik a roosty razor**.

C

crannie
The little finger of either hand. 'Oor David his mairriet intil an affa nice faimly. They aa drink their tea wi their crannies oot.'

crikey dicks!
All-purpose exclamation. 'Crikey-dicks! It's yersel. I thocht ye wis deid.'

crochlie
Frail. The 'ch' is pronounced as in 'loch'. 'She got oot o the hospital on Tuesday. They pit them hame far ower early nooadays, so she's still a bittie crochlie.' Literally, crochlie is *a disease causing lameness in cattle.*

crunk her up!
An encouragement to renewed and greater effort. Derived from the days when pushbikes were ubiquitous in rural Scotland and anyone dallying would be exhorted to pedal faster or 'crunk her up'. In farming areas of the North-east, the saying was embellished to: 'Crunk her up! Ye'll seen hae butter', an allusion to hand-cranked butter churns. Also, anyone using one of the old starting-handles to fire up a stubborn car might have been urged to 'crunk her up'. Nowadays, 'crunk her up' is not limited to cycling or cars. Any North-east boss will encourage his indigenous staff by advising them to 'crunk her up'. As in: 'Crunk her up or we'll nivver get this order oot.'

Cullen skink
A thick and creamy fish-based soup, and unquestionably one of the finest North-east contributions to Scottish cuisine. Skink is an

old Norwegian-derived rural word for a ham-based or beef-based soup. Since Cullen is a coastal town, its version of skink is fish-based, hence Cullen skink.

C

cummat
Upset or overcome by emotion. Stress is on the second syllable: cummAT. 'Ina peyed forty poun for a perm last Setterday and it's intae cats' sookins (qv) already. She's affa cummat aboot it.' 'The quinie's pet rubbit turned up its taes and dee'd a wikk past Monday. She hisna got ower it yet. Still cummat.'

a cuppa tea and a cairry-on
Standard Aberdeen reply to the question: 'Fit will we dee the nicht?'

D

daily
A noun which might refer to any daily newspaper, but most commonly means the Press and Journal, *Britain's biggest and oldest regional morning newspaper.* 'Did ye see that story in the daily the day?'

darker
A blind rage. From the younger end of the social spectrum in the North-east. 'Kylie's boyfriend got aff wi Zoë on Friday nicht. What a darker Kylie took. Zoë needed stitches.'

dash the bit
An idiomatic expression of delighted surprise. Said usually in conversation, when one party has amused the other. 'Is that really fit she said? Weel, weel, dash the bit.' A slightly less polite version is **damn the linth**.

daskie
A pew in a church. 'Darren; for ony sake show some respeck in the kirk and keep yer backside on the daskie.'

days here and there

Stay-at-home holiday. Many North-east families on a tight budget, or with no great inclination to travel, prefer to devote their holidays to exploring the delights of their own countryside, returning home each night and setting off again in a different direction the next morning. 'Far are ye gaun for yer hol'days, Winnie? 'Och, days here and there.'

deem

A woman. 'Oor Cuthbert's hookit up wi a new deem. She's nae exactly oor cuppa tea, but ye canna interfere, can ye?' A **kitchie-deem** is a female who works behind the scenes in the kitchens of a hotel or large house.

deid

Beyond redemption. 'That's you deid fin the boss finds oot.'

dell

To dig. 'Faither's oot dellin the back gairden.' Also, anyone spotted swinging the lead or otherwise idling while any form of work lies undone is admonished with: 'Hey min, that's nae dellin' (*that's not getting anything dug over*).

diary

Where cows are milked or milk products are sold. Among older North-east people, a diary is very rarely a daily journal of personal thoughts. 'I'm makkin a trifle for wir denner, Sandy. Awa doon til the diary and get a pint o double cream.'

D

dicht yer feet
Ubiquitous instruction to any visitor to make sure that his shoes are clean before he ventures inside.

dichter
Handkerchief. 'Wullie, will ye stop that sniffin and cairryin-on? Hiv ye nae a dichter in yer pooch?' Also known as a **hunkie**.

dinna droon the miller
'Not too much water in my whisky, if you please.' The miller is a reference to the grain in a dram.

dinna gee yer ginger
Keep calm. This comes from the fact that fresh-ground ginger is such a powerful spice that anyone who overindulges moves a good deal faster. Similarly: **keep a calm sooch** ('ch' pronounced as in 'loch').

dippie
Anyone with a lazy eyelid. Rather a cruel term deriving from the full expression **dippit heidlichts** (*dipped headlights*).

dirdin on
Struggling by. 'Foo are ye deein, Wattie?' 'Och, dirdin on, dirdin on.' Similar to **tyauvin**.

dirler
Toilet. Derived from the days of enamel chamberpots which, when used as intended, clattered and drummed or 'dirled'. 'Ma sister canna come tae the phone; she's on the dirler.'

dirt-deen
Exhausted. 'I'm awa til ma bed; I'm jist dirt-deen.'

D

divv
Any young woman whose hold on reality is tenuous. 'She's covered her bedroom wa wi posters o Des O'Connor. What a divv.' It might derive from the word **divot**, which is also used as an insult. An alternative word is **spoon**.

dock
Not the ubiquitous broad-leaved weed (which is a **docken**) but *the human hindquarters.* Used most often when threatening a small child with corporal punishment, as in: 'Jason, if ye dinna get doon aff that wa this minute, ye'll get a skelpit dock.' Note: in some parts of Aberdeenshire, a skelpit dock is also known as a **sconed dock**, perhaps because a baker working up a good scone or bannock dough gives the ingredients a good battering.

docken
Broad-leaved weed. Anything which is utterly worthless is said to be 'nae worth a docken'.

doh
An uncooperative person. This is probably the newest example of North-east vernacular in this book, because it comes from an eight-year-old. 'If I canna hae a sweetie, ye're jist a doh.'

doms
Age-old pub game in which black tiles with white spots are

D

abutted in sequence. Known everywhere else as dominoes. 'Get's baith a drammie, Jock, and I'll tak ye on at the doms.' Occasions great elation wherever played, so on no account to be confused with ...

Dons

Aberdeen Football Club. 'I see the Dons hiv signed anither dud.' The name might be a contraction of 'Aberdonians' or might have something to do with the River Don, one of the two rivers on which the city stands.

doocot

Pigeon loft, but also *any small cupboard or gloryhole in a house or office.* 'We keep the stationery in the grey doocot.'

dookers

Swimming costume. 'We'll hae a runnie tae Banff Links the morn. Mind and tak yer dookers.'

doon aboot the moo

Down about the mouth, out of sorts. 'Mercy, Violet, ye've surely hid bad news. Ye're lookin real doon aboot the moo.'

doon Mac's hole in America

Final response by an exasperated adult to a child's repeated questions about the location of some item, person or place. 'Far's ma sweeties, dad?' 'Nivver mind.' 'Far's ma sweeties, dad?' 'I couldna say.' 'Bit far's ma sweeties, dad?' 'Och! Doon Mac's hole in America!' Who Mac was,

what the hole was, and why it was located in America is one of the
great mysteries of North-east existence.

D

doon tae the herber

Down to the harbour. Said as a joke by anyone who finds that they
can't afford something. 'Weel, it's doon tae the herber for me.' The
implication is that prostitution is the only way to come up with ready
funds.

Doon the Toon

Totally devoid of class. 'I've jist met ma loon's girlfriend for the
first time. She's Doon the Toon, and nae mistak.' Or: 'I see Ina's got
a Spanish flamenco-dancer doll in her front windae. Isn't that richt
Doon the Toon?'

doon throwe it

Down through it is the literal translation, but its sole use is to draw attention to someone with airs and graces in speech. Anyone who attempts
to speak BBC English having been brought up with pure Doric runs the
risk of 'faain doon throwe it', meaning that he or she skates on the ice of
proper English, but occasionally and accidentally stumbles down into
the murkier yet more homely waters of the Doric. This is regarded as
a mortal sin in the North-east, akin to betraying one's roots for greater
social standing, but not even succeeding at it. 'Did ye see Mima on the
TV last nicht; tried tae lay on the pan loff (qv), but kept faain doon
throwe it?' 'Throwe' is pronounced to rhyme with 'cow'.

dother

Daughter. 'Jack's dother's mairriet Bill's dother's loon and they'd twa

D

dothers themsels.' Anyone who has listened to two or three North-east women trying to sort out any family's lineage will know how confusing it can be without my trying to explain the process.

dottled

Elderly and confused. 'Wid ye look in on Mrs Jamieson fae time tae time? She's gettin a bittie dottled.'

doughballs

Flour-margarine-and-water lumps found as an accompani- ment to a pan of mince. Like **skirlie**, born of days when meat was so expensive that it had to be stretched (made to go further). The uncooked lumps of dough are cooked as the mince simmers, and they swell in the heat. Of no nutritional value whatsoever, but their texture is curiously cloying and comforting. A doughball is also another name for *a stupid person.*

dowp

Bum. 'Her dowp's that big. If she sits on a stool, maist o't sits on the fleer.' 'Ye wid think somebody wi a dowp lik that wid ken nae tae weer track- suit bottoms.' Anyone with an especially prominent beam end is said to sport a **pelmet**. A pelmet can also be *an exceptionally short skirt.*

dowpie

Cigarette end. See **tabbie**.

dowpit

Shapeless in the seat. Any trousers or slacks which are so worn or are of such poor manufacture that they lose all shape in the behind are said to be dowpit. The word can also be used of anyone who walks with a gait which has their backside protruding. Hence: 'If Frunkie disna stop walkin sae dowpit, aa his brikks'll be dowpit.'

D

drappit
Given birth. Not a particularly attractive or respectful term for the miracle of human life, but one rooted in the farm tradition of the North-east. Not often heard nowadays, apart from among diehard Doricists well past pension age. 'Weel, loon, I wis hearin ye'll be a faither shortly. Or his she drappit already?' Travelling people in the North-east have a lovely philosophical turn of phrase for the trauma of an overdue birth. Quite unperturbed, they observe: 'Fin an aipple's ripe, it fa's.'

dreel
A row of vegetables in agriculture or horticulture. 'Foo mony dreel o tatties this 'ear, Sandy?' Note: to 'trump the dreel' is to be stuck in a rut. 'I've been trumpin this dreel for five 'ear noo. I doot it's time for a change.' The plural of dreel is still dreel.

drookit
Soaked. 'Ackie fell intae the herber last nicht and cam hame drookit.'

dubs at ilky door
Mud at every door. Doric's way of saying that everyone has their problems, secrets or faults. Another such phrase is: 'There's aye a slippery steen at ilky body's door.'

dumplins bilin ower
Used of any woman of ample bosom or who is wearing a dangerously low-cut dress.

D

dunt

A blow, but also *redundancy* or *sacking.* 'Some gawpit so-and-so's duntit the side o ma car in the car park.' 'That's me hame early, petal. I've got the dunt.'

dwaublie

Unsteady. 'She faintit twenty minutes back and she's still a bittie dwaublie.'

dwaumie

A fainting spell. It can also be used of *someone who has not been paying attention.* 'Ma mither took a dwaumie at the sink last nicht and we'd tae get the doctor'. Or: 'Davidson! Pay attention up at the back there! You're away in a dwaumie!'

dweeb

Any studious young person. Other generations would know such people as swots. Americans call them nerds. The younger North-east generation knows them as dweebs. 'Perry's that much o a dweeb that he sleeps wi his chemistry books.'

dykesider

Any child or adult known to have been conceived out of wed-lock, supposedly because their parents consummated a lightning attraction wherever any modicum of privacy could be found, usually, given the nature of North-east social life and the fierceness of the illicit hormonal rush, behind a dyke.

E

earlier bussie

Words used as deathbed consolation. Doric at its most touching. When someone's life is drawing to a close and the family is gathered about the bedside and some of the younger ones are desperately upset, the dying person usually offers words of reassurance that: 'I'll nivver be far awa. And I'll see ye aa anither day. So dinna greet; I'm only catchin an earlier bussie.'

erse

Not Irish Gaelic; this is *the backside of anything animate or inanimate, but usually human.* The more I researched this book, the more I realised that the Doric would be completely lost if this word did not exist. To give just one example, anyone who has made a bad fist of any task is said to have 'made an erse o't'. There are dozens more.

ettlin

Attempting something difficult or new. 'Ye winna achieve nithing in this warld, ma loon, gin ye dinna ettle.' 'He bocht his girlfriend perfume and a bunch o flooers fae the petrol station tae say sorry. Ye canna faut him for ettlin.'

F

face aa roon
Face all round, and so *disingenuous* or *wilfully misleading.* 'I'm nae carin if Florrie telt ye yer new frock suitit ye. Ye should ken Florrie's face aa roon.' The implication is that Florrie presents a different face to different people.

falsers
Dentures. 'I see the wifie twa doors doon's got new falsers. She's got a smile lik the Union Street fairy lichts.'

fan? / fin
When. Most North-easters assume there is no difference between these but, strictly speaking, they apply in different contexts. **Fan?** is the question. 'Fan are we gaun hame, dad?' **Fin** is the statement. 'We'll ging hame fin I say we'll ging hame and not afore.'

fancy piece
Not a woman of free morals, but *a cream cake* or *any item of sweet patisserie.* 'I'll hae fower o yer fancy pieces, baker.'

farm name

F

Phenomenon by which North-east farmers are known not by their first names or surnames, but by a shortened version of the name of their principal farm. Thus, the farmer at Barehead would be Baries, the farmer at Brownmill would be Broonies, the farmer at Bogensharn would be Bogies and the farmer at Backhillock would be Backies.

farrer up the stair

Older. An older person might say to a younger: 'Trust me; I'm farrer up the stair than you.'

farty watter

Carbonated mineral water. Perrier, Ramlösa and San Pellegrino might be *de rigueur* in the fashionable restaurants of Paris, London and New York but, I'm sorry, they're all farty watter in the North-east. 'Hey, Jim! Sees twa lobster thermidor, a ninety-two Sancerre and a bottle o farty watter.'

fash

To trouble or worry. 'Dinna fash yersel, Wullie. It's nae as bad as it looks. It's amazin fit they can shoo back on nooadays.' One who is troubled is said to be **fashious**. A minor drama blown into a crisis is dismissed as 'a fash aboot nithin'.

fat as a butter ba

Exceptionally plump. Named for the hard sweets known these days as Butter Nuts. These are spherical with a distinct blush of colour about them and could be said to resemble the face of an

F

obese person. 'What a change I see in Mary. Last Christmas, she wis as thin as a skinned rubbit (qv), noo she's as fat as a butter ba.'

feechie

A lethal concoction of hairspray, Brasso, meths and other substances favoured as a drink by rough sleepers who are down on their luck. 'I dinna ken how yon boys roon the herber can pit feechie ower their necks.' The 'ch' is pronounced as in 'loch'.

feech-up

Makeshift job. The 'ch' is pronounced as in 'loch'. 'I'd only half a pun o nails and three lengths o fower-by-two. It'll dee for a shed door, I suppose, bit it's a bit o a feech-up.'

feel

Nincompoop. 'He sleeps in a tint on the back green in the middle o winter. He wis aye a bit o a feel.' An exceptional nincompoop is a **feel gype**. The best example of its use in literature comes from Jamie Fleeman, who worked for the Laird of Udny in the middle of the 18th century and was not quite as daft as he was cabbage-looking. He is supposed to have met one of the Laird of Udny's titled friends in the grounds of Udny Castle and to have inquired: 'I'm the Laird o Udny's feel. Fa's feel are ee?'

feelin nae pain

Drunk to the point of being anaesthetised. 'We took him hame and left him on his doorstep. He wis feelin nae pain.'

F

ficher

To fumble or tinker. One may ficher with an engine, a clock mechanism or anything intricate, but there's another, more amorous definition, overheard at the back of Ballater Picture House in the late 1940s, when a frustrated young female voice inquired in the darkness: 'Wullie, fit wye div ye nivver ficher wi me noo?'

files

Occasionally. 'So tell me, Mrs Fraser, how often do your son and grandchildren visit you nowadays?' 'Only files.'

filled a holie

Filled a hole. At the end of any meal which has been judged neither too excessive nor too slight, someone will lean back and offer as approbation: 'Weel, that jist filled a holie.' The implication is that a gnawing vacant spot in the stomach has been satisfied to perfection.

fillims

Cinema. North-east Scots have a persistent inability to pronounce the word for 'moving pictures' in one syllable. 'Are ye gaun oot the nicht, Donald? The pub, maybe? The dancin? The fillims?'

fired legs

Rawness and tenderness of skin when wet clothes have been worn for too long. It applies mostly to hillwalkers and to small children pre-1970s who wet themselves at school because they were too scared to ask for permission to leave the room. 'I'm gaun up tae the school and sort oot that teacher wifie the morn. That's the loon hame wi fired legs for the third day in a row.'

F

fit?

What? All interrogative pronouns which begin in English with 'wh', begin with 'f' in the Doric. (**Fit? Fa? Foo? Fan? Fit wye? Far?**) This lends the Doric-speaker a delicious crispness when confronted by pomposity. 'You have to understand, Mr Duncan, that due to the intrinsic peculiarities of the socio-economic climate in the current budgetary period, the strictures of Government block-grant policy *vis-à-vis* local authorities entails my declining your thoroughly apposite request to have an inside toilet fitted in the abode in which you currently reside.'

'Fit?'

fit like?

How are you? The quintessential North-east greeting, by which sons and daughters of the North-east recognise each other worldwide. No matter where on the globe the encounter might take place, those two words encapsulate the warp and weft of everywhere from Peterhead to Braemar, Laurencekirk and Lossiemouth. The customary reply is: 'Nae bad. Foo's yersel?' To this, the reply is usually: 'Tyauvin.' (qv)

fit o Market Street

Sacked. From the days when the Employment Exchange was located at the bottom of Market Street, Aberdeen. 'Weel, that's me awa tae the fit o Market Street again. Lord knows fit I did wrang.' Or: 'If you're nae careful, my lad, ye'll be at the fit o Market Street in five minutes flat.'

fite

Many Doric versions of English words beginning with 'wh', replace the 'wh' with an 'f'. Thus, fite means *white*. Hence, someone observing the paleness of another person's toes, soles, heels and ankles might exclaim: 'Fit fite yer feet are.'

F

fit's yer news?
Friendly inquiry on meeting a regular acquaintance.

Fittie
The old fishing village of Footdee, now consumed by the spread of Aberdeen. Anyone who pronounces the name of this community as Footdee can be marked immediately as an incomer.

five-minute silence
Aberdeen nickname for a weekly paper. See also **squeak**.

flechie
Bed. 'Hermione! Get up oot o yer flechie this minute.' The 'ch' is pronounced as in 'loch'. Also …

flechie
Infested with parasites. 'It's high time that dog got a bath. There's nithing on fower legs mair flechie.' One of the finest characters of North-east fiction was Donovan Smith's eponymous tramp, Flechie Dode.

flee ceemetry
Fly cemetery. An item of patisserie in which sweet mincemeat is sandwiched between two squares of pastry. One need only see one to understand how it got its name. Marginally tastier than it looks. Also known as **a mucker**. You can imagine why.

F

fleg

A scare. 'The gas oven gaed oot wi a bang this mornin. What a fleg I got.' Can also be a verb: 'Ma man loupit oot fae ahen the curtains and fleggit me.' 'Well, he's aye been an eediot, Iris.'

fly cup

A social cup of tea, either at home or as a welcome rest on a day out. The fly cup is the staple of North-east conviviality and can be as simple as a cup of tea on its own or, more usually, accompanied by handsome piles of biscuits, cakes or sandwiches. The 'fly' element has nothing to do with insects, but everything – at one time in the distant past, I suppose – to do with illicitness. 'Nellie? I hinna seen ye as lang time. Now ye'll jist come in for a fly cup and neen o yer nonsense.'

foggietoddlers

Bellybutton fluff or similar detritus which gathers mysteriously in the nooks and crannies of the human body, such as between the toes or in the ears. 'Horace, for ony sake, stop howkin yer foggietoddlers in the livin-room.'

foo's aa wi ye?

How's everything with you? See **fit like?**

foo's yer doos?

Literally: '*How are your pigeons?*' A robust inquiry after one's health. Not used in polite company, because 'pigeons' is a synonym for bodily parts best kept hidden for fear of frightening the neighbours and small animals. The usual response to: 'Foo's yer doos?' is: 'Aye pickin.'

fool

Not the English noun meaning 'idiot' (that's a **gype**), but an adjective meaning *dirty*. 'Dinna eat stuff that's been drappit on the fleer, dearie. It'll be fool.' A top-shelf magazine or much of Channel 5's late-night weekend programming could be said to be profoundly fool or **orra** (qv). One of the old Aberdeen characters was a tramp known as Fool Friday. A Banffshire woman who is not particularly tidy or clean in her personal habits is a **fool maach** ('ch' pronounced as in 'loch'). Her Aberdeenshire counterpart is a **fool moch**. A moch, by the way, is also a moth.

foonert

Ground to a halt. 'I ken ye're needin the back gairden dug the day, bit I've jist foonert.'

fooshtie

Stale or *rancid.* 'That back room's needin a gweed airin. There's an affa fooshtie smell.' 'Pit oot that cheese; it's turned fooshtie.'

foosion

Vigour. 'Ye need foosion tae get on in this warld, ma loon.' Conversely, **foosionless** is be *worn out, tired* or *indolent.* 'I dinne ken fit's adee wi Mina. She jis sits there, foosionless, gawpin at the TV.'

footery

Needlessly intricate or labour-intensive. 'I'm nae stuffin mushrooms for onybody's tea. That's ower footery for ony sensible body.'

F

for

An inquiry as to what you might like. 'Fit are ye for tae yer tea the nicht?' 'Are ye for a skoof fae ma ale-bottle?'

forkytail

Earwig. So named because of the twin pincers at the end of the insect's abdomen.

forrit

Forward. 'Tak yer tractor forrit a bit, mannie; I canna get by.'

free

Not gratis and for nothing (this is the North-east). Free means *runny* or *crumbly.* 'Yer jam hisna set affa weel, Teenie. It's real free if ye dinna mind me sayin.' 'One bite o her Victoria Sponge and it fell tae bits in ma lap. Onything as free as thon should nivver hiv won first prize. Still, I didna hae my cousin as the judge, did I?'

fry

A noun, not a verb, meaning *a small parcel of fish for cooking.* Few trips to the Banffshire or Aberdeenshire coast are complete without stopping by a harbour and seeing if a fry is available direct from the boat or from the processor. Fish doesn't come any fresher. 'We gaed for a runnie tae Buckie and we've come back wi a fry for wir tea.' A boat crew will also take home a fry after a trip.

fu as a puggie

Drunk. Comes from the childhood game of marbles, in which the puggie was the heeled indentation in the sand at which the marbles were aimed. When there were so many marbles in the target that no more could get in, it was 'fu'. Consequently, when someone has had so much to drink that he has room for not one more dram, he is 'as fu as a puggie'.

F

full tae the pooch lids

Absolutely packed to bursting; literally 'full to the tops of my pockets'. 'Full' is pronounced to rhyme with 'hull', not bull. The phrase is said most often after Christmas lunch, when father leans back in his seat, claps either side of his expanding tum, and exclaims: 'Michty, I'm full tae the pooch lids.' One may also be said to be **lip fu**.

fussle

To whistle or *a whistle*. 'Fussle yer doggie back here, Sandy.' 'C'mon ref, far's yer fussle!?' Perhaps used most poignantly in the tale of the young woman desperate for a date who went to the hairdresser's especially to enhance her chances. The following morning, she was heard to remark: 'Twinty poun for a perm, and the only thing that fussled at me wis a seagull.'

futret

Weasel. Emphatically not, as most of the North-east seems to think, a ferret. The word can also be used to describe a devious or duplicitous character. 'I canna stand next door's loon. There's something sleekit (qv) aboot him; jist a dampt futret.'

fyachie

Sickly or *washed-out*. This can be used of an ill or delicate person. 'Alice is lookin a bittie fyachie the day.' It can also be used of an object. 'Jaikie's bocht a new Volkswagen, bit he's pickit an affa fyachie-broon colour for't.'

G

Gabby Aggie
Any talkative woman. 'Fit's Gabby Aggie sayin noo?'

gade
Banffshire word for any individual. 'Fit like the day, gade?' Similar to …

gadgie
Person. Also largely a Banffshire expression, although common in some parts of Buchan and Formartine. 'Look at the size o that gadgie's feet.'

gallus
Someone who is over-confident to the point of cheek or arrogance. 'She's a gallus besom, that ane, and nae mistak.' Most linguists think it derives from the person's suitability for being suspended from a gallows.

gange
Prominent chin. 'The last time I saw a gange lik that wis on Desperate Dan.'

gassed

Put at a disadvantage. 'They wheepit the wheels aff his car in the middle o the nicht, and him gaun on his holidays the next mornin. That wis him gassed.'

G

gaun

Going. 'Lettie's gaun tae tell her boss fit he can dee wi his job.' 'Abbie's gaun tae the doctor wi his feet this mornin.'

gaun aa yer length

You're pushing your luck. 'Jist calm doon, Janet. Ye're gaun aa yer length.' The implication is that you're overstretching yourself to such a degree that you're exceeding your own height. Also, anyone who trips and falls prostrate is said to have 'gaun aa her length'.

gaun yer dinger

To be very energetic. 'She did the hale spring-cleanin in twa days. She wis fairly gaun her dinger.' Anyone who is overspending is also 'gaun her dinger'.

gaur

To make or to force. 'Ye better clean yer plate now, Alfie, or I'll gaur ye sit there aa day until ye div.' 'What a sad film thon wis on the TV last nicht. Eneuch tae gaur ye greet.'

geets

Children, particularly misbehaving children. The 'g' is hard. 'I'm aboot blue-heidit wi that barrafae o geets next door.' A particularly large assortment of children is said to be 'a squatter o geets'.

G

geil't

Frozen stiff. Pronounced as 'jeelt'. 'Get oot o the front o that fire, Bertha. I stood waitin an oor for a bus and I'm geil't.' Note, one can also be **geil't raa** (frozen raw) or **geil't tae the marra** (frozen to the core). Each is as unpleasant as the others.

gettin a turnie

Keeping busy. 'Hullo, Norman. Still gettin a turnie?'

gey

Grammatical modifier meaning 'fairly' or 'rather'. Pronounced 'gye' (hard 'g'). Used frequently in the North-east's habitual under-statement. A North-east tourist might endure four hours of hurri-cane in Louisiana, in which thousands of homes are flattened and vehicles wrecked, and would phone home that night to report that: 'It's been a gey winnie day.'

gie her a turnie

To try to entice a young woman at a dance. 'That's a rare bitta stuff (qv), Frederick. Awa ower and gie her a turnie.'

gie him a clap wi a spade

A young woman being pestered by the amorous advances of a young man might turn to a third party and request such action.

gimmies

Gym shoes. 'Stop crying, Albert. The big boys flushing your gim-mies down the toilet is no excuse for your PE kit being incomplete.' The 'g' in gimmies is pronounced as 'j'.

ging
To go. 'Ging ower intae the corner and tak a run up yer humph (qv).'
(*I find you exasperating.*)

ginge
Affectionate nickname for anyone with red hair. Pronounced as
'jinj'. 'Gaun oot the nicht, Ginge?'

gink
Unattractive, unco-ordinated person, not very worldly. 'Fifteen
and still plays wi his Lego. What a gink.' The 'g' is hard.

girdle
Nothing to do with large women's undergarments, but *a flat and
heavy-iron baking sheet, usually circular, which is placed on
top of a fire or stove and used for making scones and pancakes.*
'Be sure the girdle's richt het afore ye start a bakin.' It comes from the
English griddle.

glae-eed
Ophthalmic flaw in which one eye is not aligned properly. 'She
wis that glae-eed that ye wis nivver sure if she wis spikkin tae you
or the wifie three seats back.' There's a bothy ballad with the line:
'Ae ee says Forfar and the ither ee says Fife.' Also: 'Ae ee gaun for the
messages, and the ither een comin back wi the change.'

globie
Lightbulb. 'Pit in anither globie for me, wid ye? That een's blaan.'
The poor durability and value of modern lightbulbs may then be

G

emphasised with the codicil: 'It hisna laistit nae time.' Note there was also a Globe Cinema in Aberdeen, locally known as 'The Globie'.

go
To hunger for. 'I could fair go a pyock o chips.'

gorblins
Newly hatched wild birds that are not yet ready to leave the nest. 'There's an affa racket in the reef o the aul barn. The gorblins are needin fed.' Some families use this as a pejorative description of their own offspring. 'We'd better hae a day oot at the beach and gie the gorblins some fresh air.'

graip
Large garden fork of similar proportions to a spade. Believed to come from Norwegian, as so many Doric and Scots words do. This old word is still used by surprisingly young North-east Scots.

Grannie's sookers
Large pandrops.

greetin match
A crying contest. Whenever children are growing tired or ill-tempered and their behaviour begins to worsen, sooner or later one or all will begin crying and fighting. That's a greetin match. 'Come on hame, Jim, afore the kids start a greetin match.' The phrase can also be used of a catfight between older women who ought to know better.

grippy
Greedy. 'Ye widna get daylicht in a dark corner fae Chae. He's terrible grippy.' Contrary to popular myth, per head of population Aberdeen

and the North-east consistently outstrip every other part of Scotland, bar Orkney and Shetland, for giving to charity. The philosophy is summed up best in the old Doric saying: 'It's nae loss fit a freen gets.' (*What a friend gets is no loss.*)

guffie
An Englishman or *Englishwoman.* The derivation is debated. The likeliest is that it was brought north by long-distance lorry-drivers, who were amused by their Cockney counterparts' habit of addressing everyone as 'guv', which became corrupted to 'guff'. A more modern explanation, given the immigration of so many of our southern cousins, is attributed to an English person's reputation for prattling excessively about nothing at all (guff) and for expressing unsought opinions. 'There's that mony Guffies in Aiberdeenshire noo, the Doric's lik a breath o fresh air.' Also known as white settlers. One noted academic and son of the North-east once described a guffie as 'someone who is unable to leave any silence unfilled'.

gulshach
Junk food. An all-purpose word to describe everything that is wrong in children's diet these days. Crisps are gulshach. Sweets are gulshach. Fizzy drinks are gulshach. 'I wid nivver interfere in ma dother-in-law's wye o bringin up her bairns, bit they get far ower muckle gulshach for my likin. They winna hae nae teeth by the time they leave the school.' 'Gul' is pronounced as in 'seagull'. The 'ch' in 'shach' is pronounced as in 'loch'

gype
Idiot.

G

H

half hung-tee
Lethargic. 'For ony sake, Arthur, ging tae yer bed a bittie earlier the nicht. Ye're stannin there half hung-tee.'

halved and quartered
Given a severe chastisement. 'If that grocer disna gie me ma siller back for that stinkin cheese he selt me, he'll be halved and quartered.'

ham-and-egger
An incompetent person. 'I ken exactly fit's wrang wi this company. The hale place is filled wi ham-and-eggers.' Perhaps derives from the days when rank-and-file staff had to make do with brose and kail, while the bosses gorged themselves on ham and eggs. And we all know what rank-and-file staff think of bosses' competence.

hard as Henderson's
Granite-hard. 'I've nivver eaten the wife's pastry. It's as hard as Henderson's.' Note that 'Henderson's' is pronounced 'Hinnerson's'. Great debate rages throughout the North-east as to the origin of this, and I'll be pleased to take advice. A slight majority holds that

it comes from the old Aberdeen metalworks, Henderson's, whose products, as you would understand, were pretty hard. Others point to the variation 'as hard as Henderson's erse' as proof that the other theory is nonsense. Let me know.

hashed
In a hurry. 'Canna stop for a news the day, Teenie. I'm affa hashed.'

haudin thegither
Holding together. Reply to an inquiry after one's health. 'Foo are ye?' 'Och, haudin thegither.' Also **hingin thegither** or **hingin thegither bi a threid**.

hin leg o a doo
Back leg of a pigeon, meaning *non-existent* or *fabled.* 'He says he's got a Rolls-Royce in a garage doon in Manchester, bit he says he canna let's see it because he's nae allowed tae tak it oot o England for the insurance. I think it's a hin leg o a doo, masel.' You can substitute the word **cushie** for doo.

hing-oot
A girl or young woman who is not particularly fussy about her amorous adventures or reputation. 'Now, son, yer love life's neen o my business, bit if ye keep seein that hing-oot lassie I sweir I'll tak ye oot o ma will.'

hingin mince
Lank or dishevelled hair. 'Ye'd think Poppy wid hiv pit a brush through her hair afore she cam oot. It's lik hingin mince.'

H

H

hinner eyn

The end or *the tail.* Tautologous description of the back end of anything. 'Eyn' would do perfectly well, but North-east people always refer to the hinner eyn. 'Oor Jason's got an important part in the school panto this year. He's the understudy for the hinner eyn o the horse.'

hippens

Nappies. 'He's maybe a multi-millionaire noo, bit I kent him fin he wis still in hippens.'

hirple

To limp. 'Flo hirpled hame fae the dance at three in the mornin. Wi her high heels a size ower sma, she wis still hirplin twa days later.'

hoatchin

Infested. 'No, ye canna play wi Billy Duncan. His heid's hoatchin wi lice.' Such a head might also be said to be **loupin**. There are two other meanings: a restless person could be said to be **hoatchin in his seat**. And a crowded place could be said to be **hoatchin wi fowk**, as in: 'Dinna look the road o Union Street ony Setterday afore Christmas; it'll jist be hoatchin.'

homer

Any job of work which is executed outwith the normal tax regime. 'The boy next door put in wir fittit wardrobes. Fower hunder poun, plus materials, and ye'd nivver ken it wis a homer.' Derives from the fact that most of the work is carried out in homes, not offices or yards, or perhaps because the workman is based in his own home. See also **casher**.

hudderie

H

Scruffy. Can be used of anyone who is dressed badly or untidily, but is used most often nowadays of unruly hair that badly needs a visit to the salon. 'Hiv ye nae a caim (*comb*), min? Ye're affa hudderie-heidit.'

hummin a sweetie

Learning how to kiss. 'Hiv ye tried hummin a sweetie wi Izzie?' One partner would hold a large sweet between his teeth and offer the protruding part to his intended. If she accepted, their lips would brush.

humph

A hump or hunchback. 'Peer Eb. He's got a humph lik a he ferret.' Anyone who stoops is said to be **humphy-backit**. See also **twa-faul**.

I

icicle
Ice-lolly. North-east children don't eat ice-lollies. They eat icicles. These vary from the simplicity of the ice pole, which is more or less fruit cordial frozen in a six-inch plastic tube, to the elaborate desserts on sticks dreamed up by Wall's and Lyons Maid. Whatever, they're all just icicles in the North-east. 'Mam, can I hae an icicle?' 'No, ye'll spile yer denner.'

ill-fashioned
Nosy. 'They saw the furniture van ootside the hoose this mornin, and they were roon by wi a plate o new-made bannocks this aifterneen. They're the maist ill-fashioned pair I ivver cam across.' Note: 'nosiness' is 'ill-fashience'. 'They askit foo muckle I peyed for ma new car. Can ye believe the ill-fashience?'

ill-natered
Foul-tempered. This can be ascribed to any age group, but is used most often of pensioners. 'Ye winna get yer ba back fae Aul Duguid. He widna gie a blin spurgie (qv) a worm. Terrible ill-natered.'

ill-trickit

I

Mischievous. 'I wid watch that young loonie next door if I wis you. He's got an ill-trickit look aboot him.'

intimmers

Insides. Derives from shipbuilding in which the intimmers were the inward timbers of the hull. Now refers to the insides of everything from the human body to computers. 'I'd nae a wink o sleep last nicht, doctor. It's ma intimmers.' 'I canna mak heid nor tail o this new computer we've bocht. I screwed aff the lid, bit it's aa wires and silicon chips for intimmers.'

Is *he* deid?

The curious and almost universal response to the news that so-and-so 'wis beeried last wikk'. The recipient of the news invariably adopts a surprised expression and asks: 'Is *he* deid?'

ivnoo
See **Aenoo**.

J

Jamaica
A furious tantrum. 'Could I bide at your hoose the nicht, Ally? If I ging hame in a state like this, the wife'll tak a Jamaica.' Origin uncertain.

jammies
Pyjamas, but also *extremely thick spectacles for the profoundly myopic.* A contraction of 'jam-jar spectacles', presumably. 'Michty, I hardly kent ye, Wullie. That's affa jammies ye're weerin noo.'

jandies
Yellow jaundice. 'I wid stop gaun tae the tannin salon, Denise. It's nae sae muckle a tan ye've got, mair a hint o the jandies.'

jessie
An effeminate boy or man. 'Dinna think Peter'll come oot on yer pub crawl. He'll bide at hame wi his mither. He's aye been a bit o a jessie.' The English equivalents are *nancy* or *pansy.*

jing-bang
Whole lot. An expression not often found on its own. More often

found with the word 'hale' as in 'hale jing-bang', meaning absolutely everything. 'I washed the team's fitba strip. They played ten minutes afore the game wis cried aff for bad weather, and I'd tae wash the hale jing-bang again.'

jist like hersel/himsel
Just like herself/himself. One of those statements uttered to fill embarrassing silences when being forced to appreciate someone else's family photographs and trying to sound remotely interested. 'And this is Dode and the bairns in Torremolinos.' 'Oh, aren't they jist like themsels?' (Who else would they be like?) There's also the famous tale of the Aberdeenshire woman ushered in to the front room to see the deceased lying in his coffin. 'Isn't he jist like himsel?' Indeed, madam.

jools
Jewellery. North-east women hardly ever refer to their adornments and trinkets as jewellery. They are almost always 'ma jools'.

jotters
P45. 'I telt the boss he wis a big fat neep. Now I've got ma jotters.'

jump yersel
Expression of exasperation. 'I'm fed up arguing wi ye. Awa and jump yersel.' Equally: 'Awa and tak a lang jump.'

K

keech

Rubbish but, more accurately, *excrement*. 'She put the car in reverse by mistak and backit slap bang intae the midden. She wis up til her neck in keech in twa minutes flat.' 'Nae *Big Brother* on the TV again. I dinna ken how fowk can watch that keech.' The 'ch' is pronounced as in 'loch'. See also **sharn**.

keek

Sneaky peek. Comes from the Dutch word 'kijk', meaning look. 'Tak a keek roon the corner and see fit that twa's up til.' A black eye is known as a **keeker**.

ken?

Do you know? For some obscure reason, this is applied as an interrogative suffix to an Aberdonian's conversational sentences whether it belongs there or not. 'I went oot tae the bingo, ken? I won twinty poun for a tap line, ken? We got a taxi hame, ken? Ma man wis lyin sleepin on the settee, ken?'

ken fine

Know perfectly well. 'Ye ken fine fit I mean, so dinna gie me ony o yer Mr Wide-eyed and Innocent.'

kickin

Physical assault. 'That young lad's oot o control. Somebody'll gie him a richt kickin een o this nichts and he'll deserve it.' That's the Aberdeen word. The rural word is **gyan-ower**. Note that while a gyan-ower is a physical assault, an **ower-gyan** is purely verbal. 'What an ower-gyan I got fae ma boss this aifterneen.'

kindlers

Kindling sticks. 'Awa ootside and hack a puckle kindlers for the morn's fire.'

King Lear

A dreamer or hopeless fantasist. The North-east's version of Walter Mitty or Billy Liar is named because the Doric word for a liar is pronounced 'lee-ar', so the most accomplished liar of all is the King Lee-ar.

kink hoast

Originally *whooping cough, but now any particularly hacking cough.* Kink comes, presumably, from **kinkit**, meaning doubled up. 'Mighty Charlie, ye winna be lang wi's; ye're terrible wi the kink hoast.'

kinnell

A small explosion, although used most commonly of excessive gastric wind. Stress the second syllable. 'They're blastin at Kemnay Quarry again. What a kinnell there wis this mornin.' Can also be used as a verb, hence: 'Will ye stop that kinnellin or get oot o the car?'

K

kirk or a mull o't

A church or a mill of it. If it's not one thing, it's the other. In other words, if it's not beyond reproach, it's irredeemably messy. 'Jackie's a fine boy, bit he aye maks a kirk or a mull o't.'

kist o fussles

Literally *a chest of whistles*, originally a derogatory term for *a badly played church organ*. Now used to describe anyone with a wheezy chest. 'Mercy, Sandy, that's an affa kist o fussles ye've got the day. Hiv ye got a mixture for it fae the doctor?'

kittlins

Kittens, but also small children. 'Kittlins shouldna be oot that late. It's a winder that femly's nae reportit.'

knot

Not something you study in the Boy Scouts, but simply *a lump in any food which should be smooth.* Pronounce both 'k' and 'n'. 'I canna aet ma mither's custard; it's fulla k-nots.' Flaws in timber are also k-nots.

knotty Tams

An oatmeal dish that is similar to brose (qv), but made with milk instead of water.

knype

To hurry. Pronounce both 'k' and 'n'. 'Bob's surely gaun oot wi his lass the nicht. He's knypin doon the road wi his tongue hingin oot.' One form of the word can also be used as a response to the inquiry: 'Foo are ye deein?' 'Ach, aye knypin on.'

L

lang stan
A long stand. A joke played on probably every apprentice who has served his time in the North-east, whereby the foreman would instruct the new recruit to go to the storeman and ask for 'a lang stan'. The storeman would listen to the request then leave the lad standing in the corner for half an hour or more (a lang stand) until the boy realised he had been had. A variation was to be sent for a tin of tartan paint.

lavvie-diver
Slang term for *a plumber.*

licks
Punishment. Despite protracted inquiries, I can't get a definitive answer for the derivation of this, but North-east children who have been punished are said to have been 'gien their licks'. I'll happily take advice. 'Pit doon that pentbrush and come awa fae the new carpet, Felicity, or yer dad'll gie ye yer licks.' One can also give something **big licks**, meaning to put in a lot of effort.

lirks
Midriff rolls of fat showing through the clothing. 'June weers

L

terrible ticht brikks and ticht tops. Ye can hardly see her for lirks.' 'Ay, June's fairly burstin out all over.'

loafers

Aberdeen name for mixed boiled sweets. 'Sees a quarter o loafers, grocer. We're awa til the fillims.'

loon

A boy. Strictly speaking, a loon is unmarried, but most North-east men are loons from birth to death. 'Ye're an affa loon, granda.'

loup

To jump. 'Awa and loup the pailin and cry yer faither in for his tea.' An exceptionally busy town centre on a Saturday afternoon may be said to be loupin. 'Dinna go near Aiberdeen at the wikkend; Union Street's jist loupin.' Loupin also refers to an infestation. 'I'll hae til awa tae the chemist for yon special shampoo. The loon's heid's loupin wi beasties.'

low door

Bottom-floor flat in a tenement. A prized council let, supposedly reserved for older tenants. 'I wis winderin, cooncillor, if ye could get ma mither a low door.'

lowsin time

The moment that the day's work ends. 'Tidy up yer desk, quine; it's near lowsin time.' See also **yokin time.**

lugs

Ears, obviously. Anyone with particularly prominent or protruding examples is said to have 'lugs lik pot hunnles' (*ears like pot handles*). Such prominent ears are also described as **flappers**.

Lugs-be-buggered
Nickname for *anyone with prominent ears*. 'Awa ower and see fit Lugs-be-buggered wints tae drink.'

lundies
Skipping-rope game in which two people spin employing two long ropes at once and a third child does the skipping. 'We've got ae rope already. If you wid gie's a shot o yours, we could aa play lundies.'

M

mahogany
A haircut that is cropped as closely as possible without actually being a shave. 'Foo muckle aff the day, sir?' 'Doon tae the mahogany.' A similar phrase would be **intae the quick**, which comes from someone who bites her nails so voraciously that there is virtually no nail left.

makkin on
Pretending. 'See him ower there flashin fivers, makkin on he's weel-aff.' Not to be confused with . . .

makkin on
Fondling. A common charge in the days when kirk sessions heard and punished the misdemeanours of hot-blooded parishioners. Guilty parties were noted in the session minutes as 'fornicator and fornicatrix, lying abed and makkin on'.

mangled
See **minced**.

mappie
A rabbit or, in some parts of Banffshire and Buchan, *a temper*

tantrum. 'Mappies hiv aeten aa ma man's lettuce. What a mappie he took.' **Mappie-moos** are antirrhinums, so called because they look like a rabbit's mouth and if the flower heads are squeezed, they quiver like a sniffing rabbit.

M

Mattie
Any maternity unit, but usually Aberdeen Maternity Hospital. 'Quick, officer, the Mattie afore it's ower late.'

mauna
Must not. 'Ye mauna dee things like that or the bobbies'll come and sort ye oot.'

mealie jimmie
White pudding. A six-inch melange of oatmeal, onion, lard and spices, forced into an edible skin, covered in batter and deep fried. Yet another feature in the North-east Scotland healthy-eating repertoire, but delicious all the same. When served with chips, it becomes, in chipper parlance, 'a fite-poodin supper'. Connoisseurs have been known to bypass several perfectly good chippers and travel many miles to reach the establishment which, in their judgement, serves the finest examples. I have been inconsolable since the Northern Fish Bar at Huntly shut down. The best mealie jimmies are moist and cloying when cooked or, as we say, 'sappy'. Some people refer to mealie jimmies as **mealie jerkers**. There are also **Aberdeen Mealies**, which are drier and spicier than fite poodins/mealie jimmies, but no less satisfying.

meen
The moon. A common male exclamation when spying a woman

M

bending over is: 'I see the meen's oot.' An amply upholstered example might earn: 'I see the meen's oot. And it's full.' (pronounced as in hull). Also, the moon's last quarter is noted by: 'The meen's on her back.' Some older North-easters take this as a sign of bad weather.

messages
The shopping. 'Awa and dee the messages for yer mam, dearie.' Also known as **eerans** (errands). The receptacle in which the shopping is carried is the **message-bag**.

milesteen inspector
An idler. The North-east's version of lead-swinger. It derives from a lazy person's habit of filling his days by strolling the highways and by-ways.

min
All-purpose form of address to any male individual. This is the Doric form of 'my good man', I suppose. 'Hey, min; stop kickin that cat.' 'Awa hame til yer bed, min.' 'Fit like the day, min?'

minced
Drunk almost to the point of unconsciousness. The worrying thing is that this selection comes from listening to schoolchildren, who were heard recounting a splendid social occasion one previous Friday night in which most of their contemporaries 'wis minced'. Also in regular use are **mirack (short for miraculous), stottin, guttered, bladdered, blootered, blitzed, mashed, lummed, slaughtered, roarin, rubber-leggit, wastit, wrecked** and **deein the alky twostep.** The number of North-east synonyms for alcoholic abandon is truly wondrous.

minker(s)
Person or persons of low social standing. 'That's an affa collection o minkers that's moved in at number twenty-three.'

mischanter
Mishap or accident. The 'c' is silent. 'Dinna be angry, Wullie, bit I've hid a bit o a mischanter in the car. There's watter in the manifold.' 'Far aboot is it?' 'In the herber.'

miss that hisna been missed
A single woman who has known an excess of physical pleasures. 'Nae muckle winner Hilda's past her best at forty. She's a miss that hisna been missed.' Equally: 'She hisna been neglectit.'

mochie
Grey, dreary. Hence the old joke about Noah and the ark enduring 40 days and nights of storms and finally spotting a little outcrop of rock, little realising that it is the very top of Bennachie. They sail closer and, peering through driving rain, realise that someone is perched thereon. As they draw even closer, they see Wullie, a Northeast farm worker, who hails them with a friendly wave and shouts: 'Aye-aye, Noah. Mochie day.'

mollach
To hang around or *be idle.* 'Are you still mollachin inside on a bonnie day like this?' It might derive from the habits of the mole, who knows?

mooch
To beg or *borrow.* 'She wis roon moochin a cuppa sugar this mornin

M

and me nae even oot o ma goon.' Such a person is said to be 'on the mooch' or 'on the tap'.

the morn

Tomorrow. 'Come ower for yer denner the morn.' 'I'll pick ye up at eicht the morn's mornin.' 'Pit on yer party frock and we'll ging oot clubbin the morn's nicht.'

N

nae handy

Idiomatic and, thus, impossible to translate accurately. Used at the end of a spoken sentence when the speaker is trying to lay extra stress. 'I went doon til the cat and dog home. There wis barkin and myowin nae handy.' Or: 'She won twa thoosan at the bingo last nicht. She wis in a state nae handy.'

nae sair

Not painful. Anyone who is told that her grey hair is beginning to show will reply: 'It's nae sair.'

nae side

Open and honest. 'Say fit ye like aboot Ina, bit there's nae side til her.' In other words, Ina doesn't present one face to one group and another face to another. She treats everyone the same and is admired for it.

neggish

Despondent, surly or sullen. One of the newer examples of Doric, deriving from 'negative'. 'I'm gettin fed up wi Donna. There's nae a please in her. She's neggish aboot aathing.'

N

news

A noun, obviously, but also a verb in the North-east, both meaning *gossip*. 'Mysie likes nithing better than a richt news.' Or: 'Dinna news wi Mysie; ye'll be stuck there aa mornin.' A particularly vigorous practitioner is said to 'news up': 'There's Mysie, newsin up the postie.'

nib

Nose. An unusually lustrous example usually draws comment, as in: 'Peer Wullie. He's got a nib lik a blin souter's thoom.' (*A nose like a blind cobbler's thumb.*) A sharp or pointy example is said to be: 'A nib that wid crack hailsteens.'

nichts is fair draain in / fair stretchin

A phrase heard frequently every August and February. In every circle, there is always some sad case who will make these observations on June 23 and December 23. Just humour him.

nickum

A mischievous young boy; not quite a hooligan. 'I widna say her loonie's richt coorse; he's mair o a nickum.'

nieve

Fist. Pronounced 'nivv'. 'Tak that back or ye'll taste ma nieve.' Note that when a father is teaching his young son how to look after himself in a playground fight, the first lesson involves 'makkin a nieve'.

nievfae

Fistful. 'Can I hae a sweetie oot o the jar, mam?' 'Ay, bit jist ae sweetie, nae a hale nievfae.'

nievie-nievie
Rhyme used whenever a choice must be made between the contents of two closed fists, one of which is empty. 'Nievie-nievie knick-knack. Fit haun will ye tak?'

nip
Dram. Not only does it mean a shot of whisky, 'nip' is a marvellous all-purpose word in North-east Scotland. To **nip on** is to crack along at a brisk pace. To have a **nippit tongue** is to be curt. One can be **nippit**, as in caught red-handed (nippit for speedin). And any physical space can be **nippit**, as in confined.

nippie
A waitress. 'Shout ower the nippie and get her tae gie this table a dicht.' Derives, presumably, from the necessity for any waitress to be quick on her feet.

nippie sweeties
Describing anyone who is sour or uncharitable. 'The aul boy at number sivventeen's nippie sweeties and nae mistake.'

nivver a bad that couldna be waur
Doric at its most fatalistic. Nothing is so bad that it can't get worse. Or, to put it another way: 'When one door shuts, another one slams in your face.'

nivver dee't a winter yet
You haven't died in any winter so far. Said to anyone who is complaining about freezing cold, because they are obviously still

N

N alive despite the chill. 'Ye're caul? Ye've nivver dee't a winter yet. Now, I mind the winter o forty-sivven ...'

nott
Needed. 'Ye'd better finish yer dram, Geordie. That's yer wife on the phone. She says ye've visitors and ye're nott at hame.'

nowt
Cattle. 'That's a bonnie park o nowt ye hiv there, Davie.' An alternative is **beasts**.

yer number's nae dry
Snapped at any young blade with opinions beyond his years, knowledge or experience. It comes from the days of National Service, when a raw recruit was so new that his service number had only just been inscribed. 'Be quaet, min. Ye dinna ken fit ye're spikkin aboot. Yer number's nae dry yet.' Alternatively: 'Ye're nae lang oot o hippens' (*It wasn't so long ago that you were still wearing nappies*).'

O

oot for the day
Not a short tour of the countryside, but a pejorative term *for a simpleton or fool*. 'I widna bother Elsie wi yer discussion group, yer politics or yer petitions. She's aye been oot for the day.' Also: 'Nae the full shillin', 'Ae bulb short o a chandelier', and 'Twa bubbles aff the centre.'

orra breet
Foul-mouthed person. 'Ye canna tak Mary onywye; she's sic an orra breet.'

oxters
Armpits. 'Pit a skite o something roon yer oxters, Robert; they're singin (qv).' 'She ran intae the midden and wis up til her oxters in sharn.' An **oxter-staff** is a crutch. An **oxter-up** is a cuddle.

P

panjoteralised
Blind drunk. A word made popular by the late Jaikie Stuart, of Ellon.
'I doot Erchie winna be up early the day; he wis fair panjoteralised
last nicht.'

pan loff
*A particular style of bread popular throughout most of Scot-
land,* but also *the habit of speaking BBC English when you have
not been raised to it.* To behave thus is described, rather dismiss-
ively, as 'to pan-loff it'. See also **doon throwe it**.

pannie
Saucepan and/or its contents. 'Ye'll jist come roon for yer denner.
I've on a pannie o mince.'

peeny
An apron. 'Pit on yer peeny afore ye start bakin, quinie. I dinna wint
yer new claes aa butter and flooer.' Also *a child's stomach.* 'She's got
an affa pain in her peeny, doctor.'

P

peesie
Lapwing. 'The peesies are makkin an affa racket this mornin. Surely somebody's near their eggs.'

Peter's thoom
One of the black marks behind the gills of a haddock, supposed to be the fingerprints of St Peter.

pey the factor
Defecate. Comes from the days when the only reason any farm servant would be allowed to take a break from labour in the fields was to go and pay his rent. 'Peyin the factor' became a handy excuse for anyone who needed a bowel movement in a hurry. 'If ye'll excuse me, I'd better awa and pey the factor.' The phrase is still used by people who wouldn't know a factor or a plooed park if they fell into one.

pints
Not an imperial measure of volume, but simply *shoelaces.* One is admonished to tie up one's laces with the phrase: 'Dee up yer pints.' If one's laces have come undone, the friendly warning is: 'Hey, min; yer pints is louse.'

pirn-taed
Stance in which the front of each foot points towards the other. 'The last time I saw something as pirn-taed as that, it wis clockin in a fairm close and layin eggs.' Also, **bow-hoched** means bandy-legged.

P

pirr

Banffshire-coast expression for *angry distress*. 'The furniture van cam wi her new sofa and the airms wis torn. She got hersel in a richt pirr.'

pit in

To plant. No one plants anything in a North-east garden. We 'pit in'. 'I've pit in twa dreel (qv) o Kerr's Pinks this 'ear.' 'Fit kinna carrots are ye pittin in this 'ear, Dode?'

pit on

Airs and graces. 'I dinna ken fit wye Wilma hauds sic a pit-on. Her faither wis jist a barber.' Also, **pit by** (*to lay aside*), as in: 'Ina's pittin by for her waddin. It'll nivver happen.' **Pit tee** (*to add*), as in: 'Is there a collection gaun roon for Harry? I'll pit tee twa poun.' And **sair pit-on**, a noun meaning *ill*. 'I'm affa sair pit-on wi the flu.'

pit ye aff deein

Put you off dying. Something which is so thoroughly depressing that it's more depressing than the prospect of death itself. 'Nae anither episode o EastEnders, for ony sake. That mob o Cockney whiners wid pit ye aff deein.'

pixie

Cheap rainhood. 'That's it startit spittin. Could ye len's a pixie?'

pizzers

Peasemeal brose (qv).

P

pizzies
A particular size of marble for school-playground games. Among other marble (bool) sizes were **glaissers**, **picks** and **steelers**.

play yersel
An exhortation to a child to clear off and stop bothering adults. 'Awa ootside and play yersel, loon.'

plenty watter
Anyone who is being offered water for his whisky will be asked how much water he likes in his dram. The standard reply is: 'Half and half, plenty watter', implying that plenty whisky is required, too.

plottin
Not scheming, but *flushed and sweating*. This Aberdeen City word is heard usually on hot or close (humid) days, the customary cry being: 'I'm fair plottin.'

pluffer
Originally the barrel of a bicycle-pump or a hollow stalk of cow parsley (not giant hogweed, which is dangerous) down which roddens (rowanberries) were propelled by mouth power. Nowadays any peashooter. 'No, ye canna buy a pluffer. Ye'll tak somebody's ee oot.'

plunkit
Hidden. 'I've plunkit the loon's Christmas at the back o the wardrobe. He'll likely find it fitivver.'

P

pluntit
Planted. It's also used in not particularly respectful circles to report a burial. 'Aul Tam wis pluntit last wikk.'

poggit
Stuffed. Derivation unknown, but the word is used usually of someone who has eaten too much, as in: 'Look at grunnie sleepin aff her Christmas Denner aneth the tree. Fair poggit.'

pollute
Polite. Said in order to pull the leg of someone who is doing their level best not to use slang in company. 'Mercy, Alistair, you're being awful pollute the day.' The famous story concerns the woman who was trying to explain to her posh friends why her dress was so muddy: 'On the way here, I trippit ower a tree trunk and fell sklyte among the dibs.' The joke here is that she is trying to explain that she fell 'slap into the mud'. Alas, in her desperation not to appear common, she utters this flustered hybrid Doric-English. The English is 'slap into the mud'. The Doric is 'sklyte amang the dubs'. Her attempt at politeness produces 'sklyte among the dibs'. Maybe you had to be there.

pooch
Pocket. It's often said of a grippy (greedy) person that he has 'lang pooches and short airms'.

poochie
A segment of an orange or tangerine. 'See's anither poochie o yer orange, granda.' Sometimes known as a **pap**.

preenicks

Small pins, but more usually *the needles on evergreen trees.* 'That's the last time I buy a Christmas tree fae a mannie at the pub. It wisna even Christmas Eve and the livin-room wis knee-deep in preenicks.'

press

A cupboard. Nothing to do with the Fourth Estate. 'Pit that dizzen eggs on the tap shelf in the press.'

prig

Not a self-important moralist but a verb meaning *to plead* or *entreat.* It's used most often in the negative in the North-east, as in: 'If he disna wint tae dee't, I'm nae wastin ma time priggin wi him.'

pu

Pull. Pronounced 'poo'. 'Awa and pu some carrots for the broth.'

pucklie

Small amount of individual items. 'Could ye gie's a pucklie eggs til the morn, Mrs Donald?' 'Wullie, I'm needin a pucklie sax-inch nails.' Not, as many think, synonymous with **suppie** (qv), which is a small amount of liquid or other runny substance such as honey, soup, porridge or pudding.

puddle-louper

Any small jalopy deemed barely able to negotiate a puddle. 'Thon car-salesman saw oor Sammy comin. What a puddle-louper the loon's bocht.'

P

puddocks' eggs
Frogs' eggs. Tapioca pudding. Also known as **birdies' een** (*birds' eyes*).

pyock
A small bag. 'I'll hae a bottle o ale and a pyock o chips.'

Q

queerin
Gizzard of any poultry. 'Mina, clean twa hens and tak them doon tae Mrs Duncan; she's nae feelin hersel. And mind and tak oot the queerin.'

queets
Ankles. 'That's an exceptionally fine pair o queets ye hiv there, Nellie. Are ye deein onything the morn's nicht?' One may also go 'ower yer queet' (*sprain one's ankle*). 'I wid certainly come up a Gay Gordons wi ye, bit I went ower ma queet in the Dashin Fite Sergeant.'

quine
A female person. Comes from 'queen', I suppose. Strictly speaking, a quine is unmarried, but many older, married women are referred to as quines as a gentle form of flattery. 'Fit like the day, quine?' A really young girl is 'a quinie'. 'Peer little quinie canna find her mither.'

R

rabat

To rebel. 'I've tried dressin oor Sandra in bonnie frocks, but she jist rabats.' Stress goes on the second syllable.

raffled

Anyone who disapproves of another's actions, proposals or ideas would urge them: 'Awa and get raffled.' 'Six thoosan for an aul banger lik that? Awa and get raffled.'

raivelled

Confused. 'I've got that muckle paper on ma desk I'm gettin fair raivelled.' It can also refer to an absent-minded older person. 'I think it's time grunnie wis in sheltered housin or something. She's gettin a bittie raivelled.' See also **dottled.**

rakin

See **hakin.**

ran-dan

A night on the town. 'Ye're affa toffed-up, quines. Awa oot on the ran-dan?'

R

rare

Anything which is deemed excellent. 'That's a rare new coat ye've got, Madge.' 'That's a rare shine ye've got on yer car, Eric.'

rare spikker

Eloquent orator. 'The trouble wi politics nooadays is that they hinna the rare spikkers they eese't tae hae.' A precocious child who is able to form sentences well ahead of age can also be said to be 'a rare spikker'.

rax

To reach, stretch or *strain.* 'Rax ower the table and get's the saut.' 'I spent the hale day hackin kindlers and noo I've raxed ma back.'

redd yer crap

Literally *tidy your crop.* An ornithological encouragement to get things off your chest.

redd-up

A mess and, curiously, also *to tidy up a mess.* 'Maxine, yer bed-room's a helluva redd-up. Sort it oot this meenit or I'll come and gie it a redd-up masel.'

reemin

Overflowing. 'We'd sic a lot o storms in the nicht that the rain barrel's reemin ower this mornin.' There is also an alcohol-related context: if someone is drunk he is said to be **reemin fu**.

R

returned unopened
Often said of a lady who is free with her favours. 'Hilda's oot ilky nicht and she's nivver returned unopened.'

rickle
A tumbled pile, or anything in a state of extreme disrepair. 'She peyed twinty thoosan for a cottage in Glenlivet and it's jist a rickle o steens.'

rift
Bring up wind. 'If I eat even ae slice o cucumber I'll be riftin aa nicht.'

riggit
Dressed to a presentable standard. 'Let me see. Hunkie. Comb. Tie's straicht. Sheen's polished. Yes, petal, that's me riggit.'

rikkin
Exuding smoke. Comes probably from the German verb 'rauchen', to smoke. Rikkin can also be used to describe someone who is barely controlling her anger. 'Be real careful fit ye say tae Jessie. I saw her five minutes syne and she's rikkin.' Anything which has suffered smoke damage is said to be **rikkit**. An inhabited house is a **rikkin lum**. Anyone who is in his cups is said to be **rikkin o drink**.

roadit
Fully prepared. Derives from someone being set to begin a journey or, in other words, to take to the road. 'Let me see. Passport, tickets, travellers' cheques – ay, that's me roadit.' Anyone who is **roadit again** has recovered from illness.

rolie
Home-made cigarette. 'A packet o Rizlas and a box o spunks (qv), please. I'm on the rolies noo.'

R

row
To wrap. The 'ow' is pronounced as in 'cow'. 'Dinna buy dear paper for rowin up Christmas parcels. It jist gets torn aff and flung oot.' Note that a row (a line) of anything in Doric is a **raw**. Unless it's vegetables, in which case it's a **dreel** (qv). Is it any surprise that incomers get confused?

rowie
See **buttery**.

runnie
A recreational trip in the car, usually with two couples and usually undertaken on a Sunday afternoon. Something of a North-east social phenomenon. 'Come on and we'll awa for a runnie up Deeside. We'll maybe stop for a slider at Potties.'

runtit
Flat broke. A corruption of the English word 'runted', meaning 'made the runt of the litter'. 'I took ma girlfriend oot for a meal on Friday, then we went tae the picters and finished aff at a club. That wis me runtit for a fortnicht.'

rushed
Overcharged. 'Foo muckle wis ye rushed for yer new kitchen?'

S

safties

Carpet slippers, bread rolls or simpletons. 'Ma feet's that swollen wi the rain I canna get ma safties on.' 'OK, baker, I'll hae a half-loaf, fower iced buns and half a dizzen safties.' 'Wullie wis aye a saftie at the skweel.' Be careful not to confuse the three. Note that safties in the slipper context are also known as **baffies** (qv)

sair erse

A habitual complainer. 'Dinna bother listenin tae Betty. She's a richt sair erse.'

sair-made

Pained. 'Fit's adee (qv) wi ye the day? Ye're walkin affa sair-made.'

sclabdadder

Any item of excessive size, but usually food. 'Mercy, Tam; that's an affa sclabdadder o a bradie (qv) in yer piecebox the day.'

sclap

A word which evokes very effectively the sound of someone falling headfirst into mud. 'She hytered and stytered and fell sclap amon dubs (mud).'

S

sconed dock
A beating on the backside. Used in more polite company than its sister expression, **skelpit erse**, hence: 'Come inside this minute, Alistair, or it's a sconed dock for you, young man.'

scoosher
Anything which squirts water. 'Yer new car his rare scooshers, Henry. I've nivver seen sic a clean windscreen.' 'That's me drookit again. Ye micht hiv hid mair sense that buy the loon that giant scoosher fae the toyshop.'

scour
Diarrhoea. Pronounced 'skoor'. North-east teachers have long since ceased being shocked by receiving parental sicknotes advising that 'Johnnie's got a terrible dose o the scour.' Also known as the **skitter**.

scran
Any reclaimed junk or under-the-counter handouts. 'Ye get some rare scran at car-boot sales.' 'Dinna buy envelopes; oor Gordon gets plenty scran fae his office.'

scrat o a craiter
Literally, *a scratch of a creature. Someone of extremely diminished stature and girth.* 'Fit a scrat o a craiter. Ae puffa win' and she'll be awa.'

S

scratcher

Bed. Derives from the days when farmworkers slept in straw-filled beds infested with corn lice and other such insects, leading to severely irritated skin and broken sleep. 'Weel, that's me awa tae ma scratcher.'

screwed, punched or countersunk

Disorganised or, in other contexts, concussed. 'His boss dumped anither three wikks' paperwork on his desk and now he disna ken if he's screwed, punched or countersunk.'

scud

Belt, once used for corporal punishment at school. Scud is the Aberdeen City word. The country word is **tawse**. 'I wis chaain in the class. The teacher gied me the scud/tawse.'

scuddlers

Ragbag clothes. Any garments which are past their best and are fit only for the ragbag or for gardening or DIY are said to be scuddlers. 'I'll awa and pit in anither twa-three dreel o tatties, my love.' 'As lang's ye've got on yer scuddlers, please yersel.'

seen til

Seen to. Said to anyone whose behaviour has been erratic and causing concern. 'You're needin seen til, you.'

sees or **seesa**

May I have? 'Sees yer *Beano* ower here.' 'Seesa shot o yer fitba.'

S

shade
Parting in combed hair, particularly a child's. 'Be sure ye've got a stracht shade for yer school photie, Gavin.'

shakkie-doon
A makeshift bed for temporary use. 'Yer sister and her three kids are comin for the weekend? It'll hae tae be shakkie-doons, than.'

sharger
A puny young animal; the runt of the litter. 'I dinna think that pup'll see oot the nicht. It's a sharger.' The word can also be a verb, meaning *to ruin by indulgence.* 'Stop playin wi that kitten, lass, or ye'll sharger it.'

sharn
Farmyard slurry. 'Tak yer beets aff afore ye come in for yer denner. I'm nae haein sharn aa ower ma new-cleaned kitchen.' See also **keech.**

sheen
Shoes. A single shoe is a **shee**. Two unmatched sheen are said to be **marless sheen** (*matchless shoes*).

sheetin rubbits
Literally 'shooting rabbits', but used in farming communities to describe *breaking violent wind.* 'I widna aet ony mair o that lentil soup, Dosh, or ye'll be sheetin rubbits aa nicht.'

shochle
Shuffle. Anyone who doesn't pick up their feet and walk smartly is

S

said to shochle, but the crime is at its most serious on the dance floor, where no one wants a shochler for a partner. 'For ony sake, Peter, is that you dancin or jist shochlin?'

shoo

'Shoo' in a North-east context means *to sew*. 'Mam, wid ye shoo on this shirt button for me?'

shooderie

A man carrying any small child on his shoulders is giving the child a shooderie.

shootit

Exceptionally self-satisfied. 'Ye're lookin affa shootit wi yersel, Kenny. Hiv ye found a fiver?'

shop-bocht

Ready-made. One of the greatest insults in the North-east house-wife's lexicon. 'Aathing on her table wis shop-bocht.' Any North-east homemaker is meant to have the skill, time and inclination to make jam, cakes, pies, soup and bread for herself, without relying on tins, jars or packets.

shortsome

Anything which has passed the time agreeably. 'I didna mind ironin twenty-fower sarks. It wis shortsome.'

shot

Drunk. 'We'd tae tak Wull hame in a cairtie. He wis fair shot.'

showdies

Any arrangement which rocks back and forth. This can be at a funfair (showboats) or the gentle rocking of a mother trying to get her baby to sleep. 'I canna get young Aurora tae sleep ata, nae even wi showdies.'

showies

Any small funfair which travels round rural towns, settling for two or three days at a time. 'Awa doon til the showies, Cheyenne, and see if ye canna win yersel a goldfish.'

shrapnel

Small change. 'Seesa (qv) tenner for this haunfae o shrapnel.'

sikkin

Requiring. From the English 'seeking', this is standard Doric for any request. I've been in a Fraserburgh tearoom and had the waitress ask very courteously: 'And fit are ye sikkin?' I've also heard a very angry child throw a tantrum at being offered broccoli and bawl: 'I'm nae sikkin't.'

singin

Excessively pungent. 'Awa and tak a sniff o Sandy ben in the public bar. His draaers are singin.' The implication is that the odour is so ripe that it can almost be heard.

sit-in

Not an industrial protest, but a restaurant meal. Derives from the counter assistant at certain fish bars inquiring whether the patrons wish to consume the goods on the premises or to take them away to eat elsewhere, viz: 'Sit-in or tak-oot?'

skeelie
Talented or skilful. 'Aye, ye're real skeelie at reversin a caravan Uncle Rab.'

skinnymalink
A painfully thin person, hence the playground taunt: 'Skinnyma-linky lang legs, wi umberella feet. Went til the picters and couldna get a seat.'

skirlie
Favoured North-east delicacy made of oatmeal and onions, fried in lard. Usually eaten with mashed tatties, green peas and a cup of milk. Sheer ambrosia, and totally calorie-free. Not to be confused with stuffing.

skite
To slide. As opposed to '**on the skite**' which means to have an uproarious and alcoholic night out. 'Me and Joe's got affa sair heids the day. We wis oot on the skite till five.' It can also be *a dash of liquid.* 'Pit a skite o watter in ma dram, Tam.'

skitter
An inconsequential amount, bordering on insult. 'Ye ca' that a denner for a workin man? Twa tatties and a skitter o mince?'

skittery-dick
A prune. 'Ma man ate a hale tin o skittery-dicks. He wis up and doon aa nicht.'

S

sklyte
Onomatopoeic word meant to convey impact, usually of some-one having an accident. 'She wis rinnin doon the hill, trippit and fell sklyte on her bum.'

skoof
A swig. 'Are ye for a skoof o Lilt, Alice? It's diet.'

skysie
Tight-fisted, mean. 'Can I hae a shot o yer car the nicht, dad? 'No.' 'Oh, dinna be skysie.'

slappie
Nothing to do with physical abuse. A slappie (or a **trackie**) is a *narrow lane between buildings*. 'I wid hiv catched the blighter, bit he jinkit doon the slappie.'

slater
Woodlouse or *a roofing tradesman*. The context usually makes it clear.

sleekit
Sly or devious. Another marvellous Doric word which sounds exactly as its meaning suggests. 'There'll be tears afore lang wi that new wifie as club treasurer. There's something sleekit aboot her.'

slivvers
Long dangles of saliva. 'Awa and dicht grannie's moo, Sylvia. She's terrible slivvery the day.'

slivvers and snotters
An uncomplimentary description of a brood of children whose upbringing is judged to be less than satisfactory. 'He's nivver oot o the pub. She's nivver awa fae the bingo. Nae muckle winner the kids are aye slivvers and snotters.'

slochin
Thirst-quenching. 'There's nithing mair slochin than a drink o Alford watter.' (Except on the days it tastes like neat Domestos.)

sma book
Really compact. An efficiently packed suitcase or a tightly-packed parcel is said to be 'in sma book'.

sma mooie
Small mouth. Said of any sulking child or woman. 'She's got a touch o the sma mooie.' Derives from that peculiar shrinkage of the lips whenever someone wishes silently to convey their extreme displeasure. Also referred to as **the lippie**, because the bottom lip trembles in fury or in barely controlled sobbing.

smachrie
Sweets that are so cheap that handfuls can be bought for a few pennies. You'll hear it applied to cheap jewellery, too, as an insult.

S

smeddum

Courage or moral backbone. 'It taks smeddum tae be richt coorse or richt kind', which is a direct quote from the finest 20th-century short story to come from Scotland. Lewis Grassic Gibbon's 'Smeddum' told of Meg Menzies, the matriarch of a Mearns farming family, and the trials and tribulations she faced with her feckless husband and wayward offspring.

smellies

Perfume. 'Ma man wis awa abroad on business. He stopped in by the Duty Free and bocht me some rare smellies.'

smirr

A soft drizzle or mist, particularly in the morning. 'There's a bit o a smirr comin ower the hill, bit it'll likely be awa gaun dennertime.' Some parts of Banffshire use it to describe a very small amount of liquid. 'I'll hae a dram aff ye Johnnie, and jist a smirr o watter.'

smorin

Suffocating, but used most often of a bad head cold. 'Alison winna be at the school the day. She's smorin wi the caul.'

smush

Anything which has been ground or rendered into powder or granules. 'I've pickit the best o the coal oot o the bunker for ye, grunnie. Ye're jist left wi the smush, noo.' 'If ye hidna drappit the digestives on the road hame, they widna be intae smush.' Also a term for *small change.* 'I can hardly cairry ma purse; it's that stappit wi smush.'

S

snod

Tidy. 'I spent the hale morning haein a redd-up (qv) o ma hoose and, though I say so masel, it's lookin snod.' It can also describe someone's physical appearance. 'Yer new coat fairly suits ye, Nessie. Ye're lookin real snod.' A synonym is **perjink**.

snuffie

A prostitute. 'Dinna you wander roon the herber at nicht, son. Ye'll be trippin ower snuffies.' This curious name is a fond tribute to an old Aberdeen character, Snuffie Ivy, whose reign as the city's principal lady of business was marked by her trademark drip at the end of her nose, causing her perpetually to sniff. So I'm told.

something

A drink. 'Are ye for a something?' Also known as a **thochtie**.

sookit

Adjective describing anything which looks drawn, crinkled or puckered. 'I've hid weet socks on a' day and ma feet's terrible sookit.' 'Elsie's lost twa steen in a fortnicht and she's lookin affa sookit aboot the face.' Also, any young man in the heat of a romantic clinch in a corner might be admonished with: 'Haud aff that kissin, Tam; ye'll hae her sookit dry.'

soss

A minor mess. 'Gie the table a wipe, Mina. It's an affa soss o crumbs.'

sotter

General disorder. 'Awa and tidy up yer bedroom, Jason. I've nivver seen sic a sotter.'

spad

A spade, but also *to walk in a very clumsy, ungainly manner.* 'Dod walks aawye as if he wis spaddin up a neep park.' (*George walks everywhere as if he were clumping through a field of turnips.*) It derives from the farmer's and gardener's habit of measuring everything by spade lengths, when each stride approximates the length of a spade.

spare

Unattached members of the opposite sex. 'Are ye gaun tae Shona's party? There'll be plenty o spare.'

spaver

Trouser zip or buttons. A man of powerful libido is said to be 'louse wi the spaver' (*loose with his trouser zip*). Such a man might be advised to 'pit his brikks on back tae front'. A man appearing in public with his spaver accidentally open might be advised: 'Wullie, yer shoppie door's open' or: 'Wullie, are ye sellin spunks (matches)?'

spaver relation

Half-brother or half-sister. The spaver is a trouser zip or buttons (see above). Consequently, a spaver-relation is anyone conceived by injudicious opening of same in the heat of illicit passion. 'Peggy and Jimmy were maybe brocht up thegither as brither and sister bit, tak it fae me, they're spaver relations. Their mither wisna shy.'

S

speir

To ask. This derives from a similar root to the Norwegian verb 'å spørre' (to ask). 'Awa and speir that mannie fit time's the next train.' 'Olive speired fit wye ye wisna at the kirk yestreen.' 'Will ye stop speirin things that are neen o yer business?'

speir the guts fae ...

Ask repeatedly. There's no direct translation (nor does English offer a better alternative to this descriptive Doric phrase). Literally, 'to speir the guts fae' is to ask questions repeatedly until the victim's stomach begins to ache. 'Dinna start newsin wi Dorothy, for she'll speir the guts fae ye.'

spew

Vomit. 'Slow doon yer drivin, Arnold. I'm nae far aff spewin.' Comes from the Norwegian verb 'å spy ut', pronounced 'spee oot' (say it quickly). Note that in North-east Scotland you do not make someone spew, you 'gaur' them spew. 'If ye dinna pit that thing awa, Geordie, ye'll gaur me spew.' See also **tatties ower the side.**

spew or a haircut

Describing any indecisive person. 'He disna ken if he wints a spew or a haircut.' There are other, less genteel, versions.

spewin feathers

Exceptionally thirsty. 'What an affa day o heat. I'm spewin feathers.' One can also have a **moofae o dandruff**.

spik o the place

Subject of community gossip. Anyone who has drawn attention

S

to themselves through misdemeanour or glorious disregard for the prejudices and small-mindedness of others has become 'the spik o the place'. Used most notably of author James Leslie Mitchell who, as Lewis Grassic Gibbon, wrote most disparagingly of his home farming community, leading his family to say that he had made them 'the spik o the Mearns'. Also the title of a dictionary of modern Northeast vernacular, I'm told.

spirkit
Spattered. 'I spent fower oors cleanin this kitchen fae tap tae boddim. The dog cam in fae a rainy day, gied itself a shak and noo that's the hale place spirkit wi dubs.'

spit
Short for spitting image. 'She's jist her mither's spit.'

spleet new
Factory fresh. Used to differentiate between plain, common-or-garden new and absolutely brand spanking new, which is a pretty fine distinction. It is said especially of cars. 'I see the Thomsons hiv anither spleet-new Mercedes. Far dis a bobby get that kinna money?' 'Overtime.'

spud
Not a potato (that's a **tattie**). A spud is *a medium-to-large hole in a pair of stockings or tights*, seen to best effect on an amply upholstered matron. 'That's an affa spud ye've got in yer stoackins the day, Ina.' One needs only to see such a phenomenon to understand how the name arose.

S

spunks
Matches. One does not 'strike' a spunk. A spunk is 'crackit'. 'Oor Wayne'll set the hoose on fire een o this days. He sits in his bedroom crackin spunks.' A particularly angry glare is 'a look that wid crack spunks'.

spurgie
A sparrow. 'There's nae sae mony spurgies this year, I'm thinkin.' Some older Doricists also use the word to refer to any gathering of children. 'The spurgies wis makkin an affa racket at their sports day last wikk.'

spurtle
Carved and turned wooden stick for stirring porridge. Anyone who has particularly thin and pale legs can be said to have **legs lik spurtles**.

spyocher
To cough or *a cough.* 'That's an affa spyocherin ye're haudin Ina. It's time ye stoppit smokin.' 'I'll hae this spyocher til the day I dee.' Note that the cruel retort to anyone whose constant spyochering has become irritating is: 'Oot wi't! It could be a sideboord!' (*Out with it! It could be a sideboard!*) Derivation unknown.

squeak
Any weekly paper. 'That wis a queer-like caption in the Inverurie squeak.'

stairvin
Freezing cold. Nothing to do with hunger. 'Shut that door and keep the heat in; I'm stairvin ben here.'

stammygaster

A profound shock. A marvellous Doric word which is still in regular use. 'Ma brither's run aff wi the meenister. What a stammygaster!'

stappit

Stuffed. 'We'll hae tae get the plumber oot. The drains are stappit.' If anything is stuffed to bursting point, it is said to be **stappit fu**. Many a Christmas lunch concludes with the entire assembly confessing to being thus afflicted.

stave

To sprain. 'I'm sorry, boss; I canna howk tatties the day. I staved ma thoom last nicht.'

steer

A seething crowd. 'Wisn't there an affa steer at Keith Show last wikk?' Also, *to stir*, as in: 'Steer that porritch afore it sticks tae the boddim.'

steppies and stairies

A large brood of children; the time lapse between the production of each having been more or less equal. So called because a line-up for a family photograph shows the children at differing heights, according to their ages, and looking like a sequence of steps and stairs.

stick bubbly

So there. 'My dad got a new car last wikk. It's a Fiat.' 'So? My dad got a new car last nicht, and it's a BMW. Stick bubbly.' It supposes that the

S

person whose tale has been topped has burst into tears (is bubbly) at being bettered.

stick in!
Instruction to any child to make the most of the food just presented. In the recent past, this was also used to encourage any child to study hard at school. 'Stick in at yer lessons, Duncan.'

stoonin
Throbbing. 'I've a stoonin heid wi ye playin yer drums.'

stot
To bounce. 'If you stot that ba aff my windaes again, I'll stot yer heid aff the pavement.'

stots and bangs
Fits and starts. 'She hisna lang passed her test. She's still drivin in stots and bangs.'

stovies
Another North-east delicacy, originally sliced potatoes, onions, a knob of butter and finely-chopped leftover beef, all slow-cooked together in a pan. Now made more commonly with minced beef. Always accompanied to best effect with an oatcake, some beetroot and a cup of milk.

straaberry
Strawberry. The garden soft fruit, obviously, but also used to describe the nose of anyone whose drinking habits have blessed his

nose with that peculiar purply-red hue and bulbous shape. 'Thon's an affa straaberry Dod's got nooadays.'

stretchin
Embellishing a tale. 'Rab, I'm prepared tae believe ye saw Sophia Loren on yer hol'days in Rome, bit fin ye claim she invitit ye back til her hoose for a fly cup and a news, I doot ye're stretchin.' Another suitable word would be **slidin**. One could also be **comin the bug**.

stue
Dust. 'She caas hersel a housewife, bit ony time I've been in her livin-room her sideboord's that covered in stue ye could draw pict-ers.' Anyone who is particularly weak or ineffectual '**couldna blaa the stue aff a bap**'.

stue and sma steens
Literally, *dust and small stones.* When someone makes a hasty exit, bystanders will observe wryly that 'ye couldna see him for stue and sma steens'.

stue-collector
Table ornament. So called because it serves no useful purpose, but has to be dusted daily. 'Jeannie took me hame a china doll fae Butlin's. It's jist anither stue-collector.'

stunkit
Sulked. 'I dinna ken fit I said tae offend her, but Izzie's stunkit wi me.'

S

sung
Singed. Said usually of burned food, and mostly of soup, especially soup that has been reheated too often. 'That micht hiv been a fine broth last wikk, Lottie, bit it's fairly sung noo.' Also: 'Can ye sing?' 'Ay, I've often sung the custard.'

suppie
A very small amount. 'I canna hae ony o yer trifle, Mabel. I'm on a diet. Och, weel, maybe jist a suppie.'

surely a lee
Must have been a lie. Retort to anyone who has forgotten what he was about to say. 'Ay, Charlie, that wis surely a lee.'

sut
So. Used for emphasis in an argument. 'I will not.' 'Ye will sut.'

swack
Lithe or supple. 'I'm affa sorry, bit ye'll hae tae slow doon, boys. I'm nae as swack as I eese't tae be.'

sweelie
A small libation. 'Ye'll hae a dram, Charlie?' 'Na, I'd better awa hame.' 'Come awa, ye'll surely manage ae last drammie.' 'Och, a'richt, seein as it's yersel. Jist a sweelie.'

sweetie-wife
Any effeminate man, but especially one older than 50. 'Alec's a bit o a sweetie-wife, bit he's hairmless.' Also known as a **jessie** or a **janet.**

sweir

To utter oaths. 'There's nae need tae sweir lik that, faither.' I was talking once to a Peterhead teacher of eight-year-olds who said she had asked her class what talents they thought their parents had. One boy asserted that his father 'wis a bliddy good sweirer'. See also ...

sweir

Reluctant. 'I wid fairly hae a go at sortin the mower masel, mither, bit I'm sweir in case I dinna dee't richt.'

swick

To cheat or *a person who cheats.* 'I dinna play cards wi Ackie; nae since I fun oot that he swicks. His wife's a bit o a swick, as weel.' One of the most biting satires seen on the North-east stage was one 'Scotland the What?' character invented by Steve Robertson and Buff Hardie. Cooncillor Alexander Swick was an Aberdeen baillie who was alive to every scam, fact-finding mission, expenses fiddle, free lunch, patronage and nepotism that he could sniff. Complete fiction, naturally.

syne

Ago. 'This is the same car I used lang syne.' It can also mean *then*. 'Syne she drappit doon deid, jist lik that. Nae even a cheerio.'

T

tabbie
Cigarette dog-end. 'Ronnie's fairly hit a roch patch. Ye see him doon at the herber pickin tabbies aff the pavement.'

tacket
A hobnail. 'Ye'll need new tackets on yer beets, Gordon. They're lookin gey worn.' Nailing tackets on a schoolboy's boots was a sign of coming-of-age in the Victorian and Edwardian North-east, and the lad who could spark tackets was especially feted.

tak aa
School-attendance inspector. Truancy officer. Official sent to investigate why an Aberdeen child has not been attending school. 'I've nivver been sae black-affrontit. Fa cam til the door this mornin? The tak aa, that's fa.'

tak a tellin
Heed a warning. 'She widna tak a tellin, and now she's mairriet him.'

tak a tummle

To trip and fall. Alternatively, *to take stock of one's personal circumstances.* 'Josie took a tummle and skinned her knees.' 'Dougie wis nivver oot o trouble wi the bobbies, bit he took a tummle til himsel and now he's learnin tae be a meenister.'

tak ee

Or *takee.* The North-east version of the playground chasing game, tag.

tak ma haun

An offer of support, as in: 'Tak ma haun, ma trusty freen', *but more usually a warning to a child of impending physical punishment.* 'Fiona, if you dinna stop bouncin on the settee wi yer fool feet, I'll tak ma haun aff the side o yer heid.'

tak the len

Take advantage of. 'Annie's a gweed-hertit sowel, bit that femly o hers jist taks the len o her.'

Tally

Any Italian-owned café. 'Ye'll nivver beat a Tally for an ice-cream.' Those towns fortunate enough to have had two such establishments (such as Grantown-on-Spey) usually differentiated between the two by labelling them the Top Tally and the Bottom Tally, depending on their location on the main street. The viscous raspberry sauce squirted on cappies and sundaes was sometimes known as **Tally's bleed**.

T

tap line

Pre-tax earnings. 'Fit's yer tap line this wikk, Pat?' Derives from the figure's position on the payslip. The tap line is also the most important point on the agenda for any meeting.

tap o da's egg

The very best. 'Ma quinie means aathing tae me. She's jist the tap o da's egg.'

tapper

One who tries habitually to borrow money, usually forgetting to pay back. 'Here's Aul Duncan again, what an affa tapper that mannie is. Mak on ye hinna seen him.'

target

A sartorial disaster. See also **ticket**. 'I widna buy that frock if I wis you, Janet. Ye look a richt target.'

tarry

Younger North-easters would define this as *lucky*, but the traditional meaning is *untrustworthy.* 'Dinna get ower chummy wi that laddie fae the fairm. I hear fae the shopkeepers in the village that he's turned a bittie tarry.' Also **tarry-fingert**, which presumably derives from a habit of stealing, or having sticky fingers.

tassie

A cup. It derives from the French tasse, obviously, and had fallen into disuse before Queen Victoria died, but has been revived in the last 20 years on the menus of the more twee restaurants and official functions in the North-east. In these, tea is described as 'a tassie o leaf bree' and coffee as 'a tassie o bean bree.' How quaint.

T

taste
To taint something. 'Keep the soap pooder awa fae the loaf, or it'll taste it.' One could equally use the verb **smell**.

tattie-masher
Prize marble. 'That's some tattie-masher ye've got there, Doddie.' A tattie-masher is also the kitchen implement for turning boiled potatoes into mashed potatoes.

tatties
Potatoes, obviously, but also an Aberdonian expression meaning *finished.* 'Heather, if ye dinna get that mess cleaned up afore the boss comes back ye'll be tatties.' Short for **tatties ower the side**, an expression from trawling's heyday. I've found two possible derivations for this. One group holds that it describes the act of throwing any surplus scraps of unusable grub overboard at the end of the meal. The other group asserts that it refers to seasickness, when the victim's recent meal (the tatties) would be vomited into the ocean (ower the side). In any case, the meaning of both is the same – *finished.*

Teenie fae Troon
Any woman who fancies herself as someone of style or social position. 'Tak a look at Teenie fae Troon. She thinks she's something.'

T

tee til
Next to, against. 'Jist you tak yer voluptuous self ower here darlin, and sit yersel tee til me.'

teet-bo
Very difficult to translate, but this is what a North-east adult says in a high-pitched, comic voice to a very small child when peeping out repeatedly from behind a cushion, for example, and pretending to surprise the infant. The closest English word, I suppose, is peekaboo.

tekkie
A very brief visit. 'I'll jist tak a tekkie in by the bookies.'

ten-to-two
Splay-footed. 'Oor Erchie wis put oot o the Army for his ten-to-two feet.' Derives from the position of hands on a clockface.

teuchter
Son or daughter of the rural North-east. See also **Toonser**.

thin as a skinned rubbit
And that's pretty thin. One can also be **a rickle o beens** (*a pile of bones*) or **as thin as the links o the crook** (*as thin as the arm on which kettles and pots were suspended over an old black-lead grate*).

thirled
Bound, tied. Not usually literally, but more metaphorically. 'Victor wid hiv made a great career as a singer, bit he wis thirled tae Aiberdeen

and missed aa his chunces.' 'Yvonne wastit her life thirled tae that aul minx o a mither, and now the aul besom's deid peer Yvonne's left an aul maid.'

thole

To endure. 'Dan, I've tholed yer boozin as lang as we've been mairriet, bit I'm nae tholin it ony mair.' 'I canna thole that Jeremy Clarkson on the TV.' A synonym would be **'be deein wi'**. 'I canna be deein wi fowk that mistreat animals.'

thon wye

Effeminate, of a homosexual bent. 'I feel hert sorry for Rosie. What a work she put intil that loon, and now here's him knittin his ain cardigans and bakin fairy cakes. I aye thocht he wis a bittie thon wye.' Such a chap might also be said to be **a bittie mamsy** (*a mother's boy*).

through the bree

Of low intelligence. 'I dinna ken fit wye they've taen him on as an apprentice. His heid wis through the bree lang ago.' Derives from boiling potatoes for so long that they turn into mush. The tatties and the liquid become inseparable, thus the tatties are 'through the bree'.

ticht

Suffering a shortage. 'Ma mither wid mak mair hame-made wine, bit she's affa ticht for corks.' Someone who is ticht could also be said to be *excessively thrifty*. 'Davie nivver stans his haun. He's a bittie ticht for my likin.'

T

T

ticket

One who is dressed badly. 'I dinna ken fit Annie's thinkin aboot, pittin her faimly oot dressed lik thon. Ye see some affa tickets nooadays.' See also **target**.

timmer up

To sort out or *to chastise.* 'I made a surprise visit tae the buildin-site and the labourers wis aa sittin on their backsides drinkin Dazzle. I timmered them up in twa minutes flat.'

tinkie

Any travelling person. There was no criticism or condescension in the word. It was simply a statement of fact. That is not the case with **tink**, a highly emotive way to describe a quarrelsome or sluttish woman. 'Yer mither's jist a tink,' has upset many a North-east schoolchild and has helped spark a few court cases.

tinkie's tartan

The pattern of blue veins and red blotches seen most commonly on the legs of elderly women, or on those who have fallen asleep in front of a fire.

tinkie's tae

Modern method of making tea, by dipping a teabag into a mug of boiling water. To anyone over 50, this is a sign of lax housekeeping and poor kitchen standards. Young people hoping to impress future in-laws with their domestic skills are advised to get out the teapot.

T

tint

Lost. 'I'm feart tae tell ma man, bit I've tint the ruby bracelet he gied me for ma Christmas.' The word can also feature in an exasperated call to unruly children: 'For ony sake, awa and get tint.'

tongue that wid clip cloots

Speech so abrasive that it would leave cloth in tatters. Doesn't translate well, but used to describe that breed of woman who takes no prisoners and is not shy of letting fly with ripe language in defence of that which she holds dear. 'I widna cross her if I wis you. She's got a tongue that wid clip cloots.'

took the gate

Ran off at high speed. 'I telt him I micht be pregnant and he took the gate.'

Toonser

An Aberdonian. An uncomplimentary description of a son or daughter of the Granite City, used exclusively by those born and bred in the country. 'She's fairly got airs and graces, bit she's jist a Toonser.' Correspondingly, an Aberdonian will refer equally disparagingly to country-dwellers as **teuchters**.

tooshtie

An extremely small amount, barely perceptible. 'I'm on a diet. Nae mair than a tooshtie o butter on ma toast, if ye please.' Not to be confused with . . .

T

toosties
Wire hair-curlers. 'Flora winna be minutes. She's takkin oot her toosties.'

top show
Exceptionally good. More of a young North-easter's expression than a traditional one. 'I saw ye left the club early last nicht wi thon hunky young gym teacher, Felicity. Did everything develop as ye expectit?' 'Oh, top show, Angela. Absolutely top show.'

torn-faced
Description of anyone who looks miserable.

tractor ile
Tea or coffee that is far too strong. 'Mercy, Betty, that's tractor ile ye're giein me the day.' Strong tea is also said to be **stewed**.

Trades
The July fortnight's holiday in Aberdeen in which manual workers and factory workers head for sunnier climes. 'I canna get a plumber for love nor money.' 'That's because it's Trades.'

trickit
Exceptionally pleased. 'Her faither bocht her a new party frock. She's affa trickit wi hersel.' Not to be confused with **ill-trickit**, which means *mischievous*, as in: 'I widna trust that laddie; there's something affa ill-trickit aboot him.'

trock
Rubbish. 'The sign says Antiques Shop, bit there's only aul trock inside.'

tummle the cat
Child's somersault. 'The bairn's as happy as onything; oot on the back green tummlin the cat.'

twa bob in the poun
Devoid of commonsense. 'I widna bother gettin involved wi Charlie's sister. She's twa bob in the poun, thon craiter.' Such a person could also be **short o a shillin**.

twa bubbles aff the centre
Used to describe someone who is eccentric or bordering on stupid. It comes from the building trade, and the use of a spirit level. 'Did ye see that reader's letter in the daily paper the day? Fa ivver wrote thon's definitely twa bubbles aff the centre.'

twa faul
Bent double or, more literally, *folded in two.* It can be used of paper or cardboard, but more often used of an elderly person with a pronounced stoop. 'What a peer craiter Mrs Duguid's turned. I saw her gaun her messages last nicht and she's nae far aff twa faul.'

tyauve
A struggle. Pronounced 'chaav' and sometimes spelled that way. It is used to best effect in that old North-east cry of weariness at the end of a hard working day: 'It's a sair tyauve for a half-loaf.' Also a

T standard riposte to an inquiry after one's health, viz: 'Fit like the day?'
'Tyauvin.'

U

unco
Exceptionally. 'Dinna try slidin onything past the boss. He gets unco aakward if he catches ye.'

up in a lowe
Consumed by flames. 'Did ye nae hear the sireen? Did ye nae see aa the blue lichts? Norman's shed gaed up in a lowe last nicht. Nae even a spad left.' An especially voracious fire is said to be a **blue lowe**.

up the golden staircase
Dead. 'Peer Annie. That's her up the golden staircase. Still, she's better aff awa.'

up the wrang close
Up the wrong lane. Aberdeen's version of: 'You're barking up the wrong tree.' 'Ye'll nivver guess fit she's deen noo.' 'Crashed her car?' 'No, ye're up the wrang close there.'

up the wrang dreel
Up the wrong row in the garden or field. Rural equivalent of **up the wrang close**.

V

vratch

A wicked or unkind person. 'She widnae even attend her ain dother's weddin. What a vratch.' An exceptional example might be labelled 'a coorse vratch'. It comes from the English 'wretch'.

W

waak up and doon
Futile advice to a fractious child who is profoundly bored. 'Awa and waak up and doon a while.' A crueller version would be: 'Awa oot and play on the dual-carriageway.'

wackit
Mis-shapen. Said mostly of clothes which have not stood up to washing and have shrunk, discoloured or otherwise warped. 'That's ma Sunday cardigan come oot o the machine wackit.'

Walker's Bus
The North-east version of Shanks' Pony. 'No, ye canna see me hame fae the dance. I'd raither tak Walker's Bus.' The phrase **Shanks' meer** (*Shanks' mare*) is also used.

warslin
Struggling or *plodding.* Another of those hardy retorts to the habitual North-east greeting: 'Fit like?' 'Och, warslin on.' 'She warsled throwe the day, though she'd a thumpin sair heid.' See also **tyauvin**.

waste o time gaun hame
Said of any frail person at a funeral.

watter made waur
Weak tea. Said by someone who would have preferred a plain drink of water than to have it ruined by a quick dip of a teabag and then passed off as a genuinely satisfying cuppie. 'Forty pee for thon? It wis nithing bit watter made waur.'

watterie
The loo. 'Ma mither canna come til the door. She's in the watterie readin the *People's Freen*.' Some people use the word **sitooterie** (*the place where one sits out*), although there are dangers here now that sitooterie can also mean a *conservatory*. The potential of such confusion hardly bears thinking about. People who are dismissive of the current fashion for conservatories describe them, disparagingly, as **lean-tees** (*lean-tos*), because they sit uneasily with the design of the host house and look supposedly like nothing more than lean-to sheds.

weel-fired
Baked for slightly longer than its allotted time. Anything in the baker's window which is slightly darker than usual can be said to be 'weel-fired'. 'Granda likes a weel-fired buttery.' However, in the domestic context, 'weel-fired' is usually just a synonym for charcoal, despite the fervent denials of the home-baker. 'Ma rock cakes are nae brunt. They're jist weel-fired.'

weel on
Drunk. 'Dinna gie Sandy anither dram, barman. He's weel on as it is.'

weersis

Our or ours. North-east child's attempt at the English plural possessive. I used to think this was a simple misunderstanding by one or two children, but I've since heard it so frequently and in so many villages that it must have become part of the idiom or dialect. 'Come and see weersis new car.'

weldies

Wellington boots. 'Pit on yer weldies and come and help in the gairden.'

went

Aberdeen city's past tense of the English verb 'to go'. 'Far's Julian?' 'He's went hame.' In the rural hinterland, the equivalent word is 'gaen'.

the wheels fell aff

Idiomatic expression to bring down to earth someone who brags about possessions or who has ideas about his/her station. 'I've got a lovely Indian writing-desk from the pre-Raj period in ebonised amboyna. Found it at a little antique shop in the Old Town. It was a snip. The owner clearly didn't know what a treasure he had. I felt almost guilty at the pittance I paid for such a lovely piece.' 'Aye, we'd een o them bit the wheels fell aff.'

wheepit

Whipped. Could be used of cream, I suppose, but more often used to express speed. 'The car wheepit through the village at an affa lick.' 'She'd wheepit the sark aff him afore he'd time tae say no.'

W

whoop-de-do
Supposed expression of delight, but dripping with sarcasm. 'I see we're gettin anither ten-poun Christmas Bonus this 'ear. Whoop-de-do.'

Widdie
A small wood, but also *a generic term for any cheap cigarette.* Derived from that old favourite, the Woodbine. 'Ony Widdies on ye, Tam? I'm gaspin.'

widna bother ma erse
I have no intention of troubling myself.

Wiggy Jim
Any judicial person wearing a wig, but most often used of the sheriff at a sheriff court. 'The Wiggy Jim said he wis awardin ma wife fifty poun because she'd putten up wi ma bad behaviour for sae lang. I said I wid see if I could chip in a coupla quid masel.'

winnie
Good fortune. A North-east person does not win a raffle; does not win at the bingo and does not win the Lottery. She 'has a winnie'.

wint
A lacking in the IQ department, worryingly eccentric or simply vacant. 'Hiv ye seen the new boy in the General Office? There's a wint there.'

wired up wrang
Describing anyone whose behaviour is aggressive or plain

stupid. 'A walk doon Union Street on a Friday nicht shows ye that young fowk nooadays are jist wired up wrang.'

wirds are win'
Words are wind. Of all the phrases which came my way during the researches, this was the one which summed up North-east philosophy most neatly. Words are worthless, it's actions that count. 'Tony Blair? A moofae o teeth spewin fine wirds, bit wirds are win'.' A similar homily would be **Fair wirds winna bile the pot** (*fair words won't cook anything*).

wrang spy
Wrong guess. An Aberdeen expression said to any child who has picked hastily or answered wrongly. 'Fitna haun's the sweetie in?' 'That een.' 'No; wrang spy.'

W

Y

yackered
Exhausted. A marginally more genteel form of **knackered**.

Ye see it aa
You see it all. One of the customary responses to the definitive Doric greeting, 'Fit like?' As in: 'Fit like the day?' 'Ach, ye see it aa.' It has an air of dejection about it, as if the respondent is not entirely happy with herself and considers herself not worth the attention.

Ye widna need tae be . . .
You wouldn't need to be. Many sentences begin with these words, implying frustration or resignation. For instance, if two people have waited for half an hour for a bus service which is supposed to run every ten minutes, they might say: 'Ye widna need tae be in a hurry.' If someone has just seen a belligerent drunk ushered from her company, she might observe philosophically: 'Ye widna need tae be easy offendit.' And so on.

Ye'll catch flees
A gentle suggestion to anyone who is wandering around with his

mouth open, the implication being that unless he shuts it, he will swallow insects.

Ye'll ken me next time

Statement delivered vigorously by someone who feels that a passer-by has been staring at him. In similar circumstances, anyone who asks: 'And fit are ee starin at?' might be treated to the reply: 'Lord knows; the ticket's faan aff.'

Ye're at yer untie's

Literally, *you're at your aunt's house.* This idiom is still in frequent use whenever a child is urged to help himself to food on the table while visiting someone else's home, whether or not the hostess is an aunt. 'Come on noo, young Simon, aet up; ye're at yer untie's.' The extended version implies that the hostess cannot see what is being eaten, so it wouldn't matter in any case how much the child consumed: 'Ye're at yer untie's and she's blin.'

yestreen

Yesterday or *last night.* The exact meaning depends on the age of the person using the word. An elderly North-easter will use yestreen to mean 'at any point yesterday'. A middle-aged one will mean 'last night, from about 6 p.m. or later'. 'Did ye ging oot tae the pub yestreen?' 'Wis thon nae an affa day o win' yestreen?' Often, the 'y' is not pronounced.

yokie

Feeling itchy. 'I've affa yokie feet.' Also, a peculiar form of cruelty perpetrated among schoolboys. The assailant rushes up behind the

Y

victim, clutches the victim's hips, thereby locating the sides of the victim's underpants. Still gripping the underpants, the assailant tugs sharply upwards, compressing the victim's reproductive accoutrements with such speed and pressure that the pain is truly excruciating. The victim, now with tears in his eyes and his stomach in his throat, has just been treated to 'a yokie'.

yokin
The act of relieving an itch, or *scratching*. 'Tam, will ye stop yokin aboot yersel in public? Fowk'll see.' It comes from an old Dutch verb, 'jeuken'. Synonymous with **howkin** and **claain**. Not to be confused with . . .

yokin time
Not an interval set aside for relieving itches, but *the moment that the day's work starts*. 'Yokin time's sivven o'clock the morn's mornin, boys.' See also **lowsin time.**

youse
The plural of you. This is another Glaswegian speech abomination creeping into urban Doric and roundly despised by rural Doricspeakers, who see it as another example of a lack of class. 'Are youse aa comin tae the pub the nicht?' Part-time waiters can be heard in many Aberdeen establishments inquiring: 'What can I get youse, guys?' More than one rural Doricist has suggested drily that Toonsers might benefit from a special section in Hallmark shops, with cards bearing the wish: 'Happy Birthday To Youse.'

Z

zatny affa?
Isn't that terrible? Expression used by anyone seeking conversational agreement about how despicable something is. 'The bank charged forty poun tae close ma deid uncle's accoont. Zatny affa?' The standard reply is: "At's affa, 'at.'

Zube
A fool. A middle-aged person's expression, deriving from the old cough sweet, for anyone who is devoid of commonsense. 'Dinna believe fit Jim telt ye. Jim's jist a Zube.'